teach®
yourself

business plans

D0785170

business plans
polly bird

For over sixty years, more than
40 million people have learnt over
750 subjects the **teach yourself**
way, with impressive results.

be where you want to be
with **teach yourself**

For UK order enquiries: please contact Bookpoint Ltd, 130 Milton Park, Abingdon, Oxon OX14 4SB. Telephone: +44 (0)1235 827720. Fax +44 (0)1235 400454. Lines are open 09.00–18.00, Monday to Saturday, with a 24-hour message answering service. Details about our titles and how to order are available at www.teachyourself.co.uk

For USA order enquiries: please contact McGraw-Hill Customer Services, PO Box 545, Blacklick, OH 43004-0545, USA. Telephone: 1-800-722-4726. Fax: 1-614-755-5645.

For Canada order enquiries: please contact McGraw-Hill Ryerson Ltd, 300 Water St, Whitby, Ontario L1N 9B6, Canada. Telephone: 905 430 5000. Fax: 905 430 5020.

Long renowned as the authoritative source for self-guided learning – with more than 40 million copies sold worldwide – the **teach yourself** series includes over 300 titles in the fields of languages, crafts, hobbies, business, computing and education.

British Library Cataloguing in Publication Data: a catalogue record for this title is available from the British Library.

Library of Congress Catalog Card Number: on file.

First published in the UK 2004 by Hodder Arnold, 338 Euston Road, London, NW1 3BH.

First published in the US 2004 by Contemporary Books, a Division of the McGraw-Hill Companies, 1 Prudential Plaza, 130 East Randolph Street, Chicago, IL 60601 USA.

This edition published 2004.

The **teach yourself** name is a registered trade mark of Hodder Headline Ltd.

Typeset by Servis Filmsetting Ltd, Manchester
Printed in Great Britain for Hodder Arnold, a division of Hodder Headline, 338 Euston Road, London NW1 3BH, by Cox & Wyman, Ltd, Reading, Berkshire.

Hodder Headline's policy is to use papers that are natural, renewable and recyclable products and made from wood grown in sustainable forests. The logging and manufacturing processes are expected to conform to the environmental regulations of the country of origin.

Impression number   10 9 8 7 6 5 4 3 2 1
Year   2010 2009 2008 2007 2006 2005 2004

contents

Dedication

To Tony Sproston and his team, with thanks.

A business plan is one of the most important documents that anyone starting a business or running one needs to produce. It is not only a potential leverage for loans or investment by others but also a guide to how you hope your business will develop. It is the document that potential investors will expect to see and can make or break your chances of getting money or other kinds of aid for your business.

It is perhaps not surprising therefore that for many people the idea of producing a business plan creates panic. You might be one of those people. You know you need a business plan but are not sure what it is or how to set about producing one. If you do have an idea of what to put in one, you might be unsure of how it needs to be set out or whether you have put in too much or too little or whether the content is relevant. The problems don't stop there. Once you have got one, what do you do with it? Is its job over once you have shown it to a bank manager or potential investor?

What this book will tell you

This book aims to remove the fear from creating a business plan. It sets out why you need a business plan, what to put in it and how to present it. It ensures that you understand the kind of business you have or hope to have, and gives advice on how the plan can be used once the business is up and running. It does not assume any prior knowledge and aims to ensure that you acquire a thorough understanding of each section. You cannot complete a business plan without including financial information, but this is kept to a minimum to keep it simple. There are tests, checklists and questionnaires to help you consolidate your knowledge and a helpful Taking it Further section at the end. By the time you have read this book, you should be able to produce a basic business plan.

Before you can write a business plan you will need to do a lot of basic research about your business or proposed business. You need to understand your business thoroughly before you can explain it to others. You will need a lot of background information so that you can provide the necessary details in your plan. This book will explain what areas of your business you need to find out about, why they are important to your business and why they need to go in your plan. By finding out how your business should work you will not only get the necessary background information but will have a better understanding of your business. That will help you run your business more effectively.

Who needs this book?

You need this book if you want to start a new business and need money or other help to make things happen. If you already run a business you need a plan to get money or help for improvements, expansion or plant. All businesses need plans to help them run more effectively and to suggest future development. Students will find this book useful as a basic guide to business plans and an informative and interesting introduction to the basic issues of running a business. Business plans are also useful planning tools for charities, public sector bodies and other types of organizations. The general reader will gain an insight into the problems of businesses, all the more important as businesses affect so much of our lives.

Using this book

This is a working book. Read it through once to get an understanding of the shape and processes of creating a business plan. Then read each chapter carefully, making notes about your own business as you go along. Study the checklists, do the exercises, answer the questionnaires. These will help you understand the issues in each chapter. Make a list of the subjects where you have gaps in your knowledge. Decide how you will do the research to fill those gaps. That might mean talking to experts, reading documents, consulting organizations or government agencies. Then, using your research and your own knowledge of the business, write a draft of the relevant section of the plan. Work out what the costs will be where necessary and record them accurately. You will then be ready to create your own plan.

After reading this book some of you might still prefer to ask a professional to draw up a plan for you. That is fine; reading this book will ensure that you have done all the necessary research about your business and can provide all the necessary data to whoever you employ to create the plan. Your input will still be vital to the plan's success.

Present or future business

You might already have a business that you are hoping to change or for which you hope to achieve investment. Or you might be trying to start a new business. As it would be awkward to write, and read, a book in which the text jumps between both types, I will generally assume that readers are starting a new business. However, remember that the advice applies just as much to owners of existing businesses.

After the plan

Just as your business will mature and change, so will your business plan. You will need to keep your plan updated so that you have a clear guide to how it should progress and can see where changes and improvements need to be made. You may also need extra help and finance at a future time. Creating a business plan then is an ongoing mission and this book should be on hand as a continuing source of reference.

'I think business is very simple.'

(Bill Gates, 1993)

Note

An example of a business plan (Acme Consulting) is provided at the end of this book. It cannot be reproduced or used as it stands but will show how a business plan is put together. Business plans vary according to the type, size and complexity of the business concerned as well as the requirements of any organization approached for aid. The Taking it Further section also includes links to some websites that include free business plan templates. Alternatively the organization you wish to approach with your plan might provide you with the plan format it wishes you to follow.

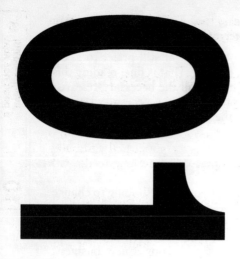

01
why you need a business plan

In this chapter you will learn:

- what a business plan is
- why you need a business plan
- how to decide who sees the plan
- how to decide who writes the plan
- how to discover what skills you need

A business plan is a vital business tool. This chapter will explain why you need one, who will see it and where you can go for advice.

Make a friend of your business plan

The words 'business plan' often make people nervous. They are unsure of what a business plan is, don't really understand what it is for and certainly have only a hazy idea about what goes into one. They have a vague idea that it is a complicated and bulky document but prefer to pretend that it has nothing to do with them.

A business plan should play an important and necessary part in any business success. It is nothing to be scared of. Taking the time to discover what a business plan is and how it can help you will prove invaluable and give you confidence about running your business. So what is a business plan?

What is a business plan ?

A business plan is a document that describes your business in detail and suggests how it might progress in the future. It shows what actions need to be taken immediately and which are long-term issues. It is therefore something that can not only be used for a short-term situation, such as raising finance for a particular project, but also as a guide to how the business should progress. It normally contains information about what the business is, how it will operate, how the product or service will be marketed and the present and future financial position. It shows what the business can do and what you want the business to do in the future. Common areas covered in business plans include:

- description of the product or service
- type of business
- management
- marketing
- operation
- finances
- objectives/goals

Each plan will be tailored to the specific business or proposed business being considered and will vary according to the importance of the situation. One thing is clear: people who make business plans are more successful than those who don't because they have a better understanding of their business and how they want their business to develop. Time taken to prepare a business plan is never wasted.

A business plan is a detailed description and assessment of a business from idea to execution that provides a blueprint for future action.

Types of plan

There are two main types of plan. First, a short-term plan aimed at getting a loan, investment, grant or other kind of aid. Second, a long-term plan that will help you develop your business and provide a blueprint for progress that will motivate staff and guide managers. Both types of plan have the same basic core of vital information, but a short-term plan will focus on the need for financial help while the long-term plan will provide more information about the business's long-term aims. In practice, the difference between the two is more to do with length and emphasis than content. Any plan should contain enough information to explain the business in enough detail to encourage investors or lenders and that in itself is the basis for long-term planning.

What a business plan cannot do

Having told you how important a business plan is to any business, I must now warn you what a business plan cannot do. However good your plan is, it can't make decisions for you. The plan is a guide to future action, but only you and your colleagues can make decisions about the business. The plan is therefore only as good as the people who implement it. You can base decisions on the plan but you won't find all the answers there. The plan cannot solve any problems; it can only identify them and suggest how they might be solved. You therefore need to be adaptable so that, if your business moves in a direction not covered by your plan, you are ready to decide what to do.

Nor can a business plan predict the future. It can forecast what might happen based on existing information, but it cannot tell you exactly what will happen. If you do your research and base your forecasts on reliable information, you can provide a picture of a likely scenario, but only time will tell how close the plan is to reality. Both you and the plan need to be adaptable.

Also, you can't make the information better than it is. 'Garbage in, garbage out' is not only the self-evident rule for programming computers but for producing any plan. The content of your plan will only be as good as the information put into it and the skill of the writer.

What is a business plan for?

You may not see the immediate point of a business plan but are aware that in some business situations it is asked for. For example, you may know that a bank might want to see one if you want to raise money for your business. But there are many reasons for producing a business plan and some or all of them will apply to your business.

Obtaining financial backing

Both new and existing businesses can have a need for money, and a business plan will show why investing in your business will be profitable. The kind of financial help you might want could be:

- long-, medium- or short-term loans, for example from banks
- permanent investment, for example, through providing shares as a limited company
- grants

You might need to decide before you complete this part of the plan what sources of finance you will approach. These might be:

- banks
- private investors
- Enterprise Investment Scheme
- government grants or loans
- Small Firms Loan Guarantee Scheme
- shares to the public
- Prince's Youth Trust
- private loans
- finance houses
- factoring

(See Taking it Further for information about the organizations mentioned.)

Your local trade and business organizations will be able to give advice about getting started with your business. Try contacting your local Business Link or local Enterprise agencies. There are also government organizations and other agencies – public, private and voluntary – that can provide advice and help for new and existing businesses (see Taking it Further).

Applying for grants

Grant providers will use a business plan to judge whether giving you a grant would be worthwhile. The plan will show that you and your business will satisfy the grant awarder's policy.

Showing that a new business is viable

If you are starting a new business, you will need to show potential backers what your business involves and that it will pay. It will show how likely the business is to succeed and reassure investors or lenders that the business will not go bankrupt and will make a profit. Anyone providing financial assistance will need to know that your business can repay any money and can sustain interest payments.

Helping people become self-employed

Anyone wishing to become self-employed should produce a business plan whether they need immediate financial assistance or not. Not only will it concentrate thinking on how the business will work and highlight potential problems, but it will show whether working for oneself is a practical option.

Discovering strengths and weaknesses

By writing a business plan you can see where there are potential or existing problems as well as where the strengths of the business lie. For example, compiling a business plan might highlight a lack of certain skills in managers or employees. A useful tool for this is the SWOT analysis which will be explained in Chapter 3.

Encouraging partners

A good business plan will encourage people to join you as partners in your business. It will show that they will be taking part in a venture with a future.

Guiding employees

The plan can be used to show employees the direction of the business and to enlist their help with the plan's execution. It can also be used to keep employees informed of changes and therefore boost their morale.

Helping you make decisions

With the detailed information about your business at your fingertips, you can make informed decisions quickly and confidently. You will be able to make better decisions immediately, rather than have to gather the background information once the problem has arisen.

Blueprint for future action

A good business plan provides an ongoing guide to how the business should progress. It helps you manage the business efficiently and is a map for progress.

Improving internal management communication

The better understanding managers have of the business the better they can communicate between departments. Managers need to know how the business works on a day-to-day basis. A business plan will show up any badly managed areas of an existing business or potential managerial problems for a new business.

Pinpointing areas for development

Writing a plan can highlight areas which it would be profitable to develop.

Highlighting problems

The plan will not only show where immediate problems need dealing with but will show where future problems might occur. This will help reduce a 'fire-fighting' approach to problems and therefore save time, energy and money.

Planning resources

Your plan will enable you to see what resources you need and be able to plan for them. You should therefore not be caught unawares by lack of resources at any future point.

Getting ahead of the competition

Any business plan needs to demonstrate an understanding of your competitors and their strengths and weaknesses. By researching this you will have a plan that gives you the tools to market your product or service in ways that will overcome competition.

Making the best use of what is available

Even if your business does not have everything that ideally it should have, by creating a plan you will be able to see clearly what its assets are and so be able to make the best use of them.

Analysing the viability of a new product or service

Creating a business plan gives you the opportunity to research the viability of a new product or service and to see how it will fit into the prevailing business market. A plan will help you uncover any previously unnoticed flaws in the processes of creating a product or service and getting it onto the market.

Providing a personal long-term guide to progress

By referring to the plan you can see where the business is deviating from this and make adjustments accordingly. It can also be a motivational tool by demonstrating where and when your business has progressed according to the plan.

Providing an overall view of the business

You might be so closely involved in your business that you do not see the overall picture. Preparing a business plan will make this clearer and provide an overview.

Concentrating your thinking

A business plan will make you think carefully about your ideas and view them as other people will see them. It will enable you to solve problems that the plan throws up before readers see it.

Impressing buyers

This is an overlooked reason for providing a business plan, but potential buyers of a business will want reassurance that the business is viable and is likely to continue making a profit. It will also give them a detailed breakdown of how the business operates.

Getting regulatory approval

If your business will require approval from a regulatory body then the plan will show the body that the business meets all the necessary criteria.

Using your plan

Your business plan could be put to all these uses throughout the life of your business. It is important to recognize that a business plan is not just something that should be created and then ignored. It needs to be regularly looked at so that you can keep track of how well your business is doing and what you need to do to keep it on track.

If it is to be used rather than simply produced and then discarded after a few weeks a business plan needs to be:

- simple
- accurate
- useful
- realistic

Bear these points in mind as you read through the book. Just because you need to put a certain amount of information into a business plan does not mean that it should be complicated or unreadable. An accurate, clearly presented plan giving the required amount of information according to the circumstances will be the most useful document.

At various stages in the life of your business you may need to create new business plans for specific purposes or to update an original one. Just putting your ideas onto paper or computer can help to firm them up and inspire new ideas. Above all, a business plan is your guide to your business's future. It needs to show where your business is now, what its objectives are and how it will attain those objectives. Chapter 11 discusses in more detail how to use your business plan.

Who sees your plan?

You might wonder who will get to see your business plan. It might surprise you to know that there are many people or groups of people who will ask for one or who would find it useful. The most obvious are:

- you and your employees/work colleagues
- bank manager/other lenders
- grant providers
- investors
- business advice organizations
- buyers
- potential partners

You will see the plan and you should share it with your work colleagues or employees. If they understand how the business is supposed to work and progress they will be encouraged to help the process. They might also have suggestions about ways to improve on the procedures and product or service. Advice from people who have first-hand experience of the way your business actually works is invaluable. If you are intending to start a business and have potential partners or employees then you can show the plan to them.

Your bank manager, grants providers and investors will want to see evidence that you understand the product or service you sell and that you have carefully evaluated the prospects of your business. You might also show your plan to business advice organizations so that they can help you improve it or give other advice.

When you know who will see the plan you will be able to tailor its content and presentation to their needs.

Who writes the plan?

You should now be convinced of the importance of creating a business plan, but who will be responsible for writing it? Obviously, the better the creator knows the business the more reliable and convincing the plan will be. People who might write the plan include:

- you
- you and your business partners
- you and your employees
- accountant
- business consultant
- business plan preparation service

The best person to write it is obviously yourself, and it can often work well if you join forces with your employees or business partners. There are advantages in preparing your business plan yourself. First, you will most likely be presenting it to a lender or investor yourself. If you have prepared the plan you will know the contents better than anyone else. You will be able to play up the strengths of the proposal. Second, you can see which sections need fine-tuning and can adjust them accordingly. By doing this yourself you can quickly adapt the plan to changing needs.

It is sensible to prepare at least a first draft yourself, if you can, and then get an expert to prepare a suitable final version. A first draft ensures that you get the ideas that you consider important down on paper. It gives you a basis for discussion with a professional who can bring an objective eye to it.

You might decide that you would prefer a professional business plan writer or someone else to prepare the plan for you. An accountant or a business consultant, given the relevant information, will create a business plan for you but they will charge for doing so. If you are starting a new business this may well be out of your financial range. There are also a number of individuals and agencies who provide a business plan preparation service.

When you are deciding who will be responsible for creating and recording the business plan, bear in mind what it will be used for and the time available. You might, for example, think it worthwhile to employ a business plan preparation service if you are starting a new business and want to impress a bank manager. If you want a personal guide for an existing business you might create one yourself.

There are computer programs to help with the creation of a business plan but they cannot write the plan for you.

When to start your business plan

Many people make the mistake of starting a business plan too late in the process of setting up a new business. The right time to start is as soon as you have decided on the product or service you want to provide and the kind of business you want to run. Collect as much information as possible from as many up-to-date sources as possible and store it in an easily accessible and organized way. Arranging the information by this book's chapter headings, for example, will help you keep the information in the correct order for writing your plan. When you come to writing up the plan (see Chapter 10) you will need to have all the information close to hand.

BUSINESS PLAN TIP
Write draft paragraphs for each section as you do your research. You can always alter it later, but a draft will concentrate your thinking and show where further research is needed.

Research – the key to success

The success of your plan will depend on the quality of your research. You can collect information from:

- banks
- government, e.g. DTI
- business organizations, e.g. Enterprise Agencies
- books
- internet
- interviews with business people
- franchiser (if relevant)
- trade organizations
- business/trade journals

Gathering the relevant information can take time so do not leave it until just before you have a date with the bank manager or an investor. If you are preparing a business plan for an existing business you will be aware of the main organizations and individuals who can help you. Allocate some time during the working day specifically for contacting them.

Internet as a research tool

The internet is now the first place to look for information. Many businesses, companies, banks, government bodies, trade associations and other organizations have a web presence with their own websites containing much useful information. However, there are risks with using internet information alone. Anyone can post information on the internet so you need to ensure that you access reliable sites. Websites produced by well-known organizations will be reliable. If you don't know the company's reputation, check their details in a yearbook or trade directory at your local library or phone their industry body. Check that information is up-to-date by looking for the date that the website was updated. Look for contact details and check the names of the organization's owners. Look at the press section of the site, if there is one, and see when the latest release was produced. This is a good place to find the latest company news.

On the internet you can find not only information about individual companies but industry and trade news, relevant international and worldwide information, facts and figures and advice. For example, the major banks have websites devoted to small businesses with advice on setting up and running them and help with preparing business plans (see Taking it Further).

Starting actions

Here are a few ideas to help you get ready to do the necessary research to write your plan:

1 Make a list of all the organizations, people and other possible sources of information. You can add to this as you get ideas from reading this book.
2 Create a timetable for making contact or doing desk research.
3 Keep a note of references and contact numbers as you go along.
4 Sort your research into broad categories as you go along – use the chapter headings in this book to help you.

What skills do you need?

You might be daunted by the prospect of creating a business plan and wonder what skills you need to do so. Do not be put off from writing one yourself. This book will show you what needs to go into the plan, and Chapter 10 will tell you how to put one together from the information you have. As long as you are methodical and realistic, writing a business plan should be well within everyone's capabilities.

Apart from writing the plan you might want to assess what skills you have for running a business. It is no use writing a brilliant business plan if you do not have or know how to obtain the necessary skills. Here is a handy checklist of useful skills for creating and running a business. By checking the yes or no answers you will see at a glance which skills or experience you are lacking. You can then either get training in missing skills, perhaps at an evening class, or decide to employ people with the necessary skills. If you have or intend to have a business partner they should do the test too. If there are clear gaps when the lists are compared then you know where the skills shortage will lie.

Skills checklist

	Yes	No
1 report writing		
2 information technology		
3 bookkeeping/accountancy		
4 marketing		

  5 public speaking
  6 management
  7 specific product/service skills
  8 leadership
  9 time management
  10 project planning

You now know what a business plan is and why you need one.
You should also have a clear idea of your intended audience and
which skills you or your colleagues need to acquire. Now you are
ready to start creating your plan.

Personal attributes for new businesspeople

If you are starting a new business it will be helpful if you analyse
your personal attributes and find out whether you are really suited
to starting a new business and in some cases working alone. Many
people make the mistake of thinking that personality does not
count, but your personality will determine the type of business with
which you will be successful. Obviously, matching your personal
skills to the type of business will work best, although if you are prepared to cultivate personal traits sometimes this can be overcome.
You can also employ people with the personality traits you lack. So
if you thrive as a backroom operator you can employ someone else
to meet and greet customers or negotiate with suppliers. Answer
the following questionnaire and decide whether you can make it:

Questionnaire
Tick the appropriate columns for each type of personality trait you
think you have.

	Yes	No	Could become
1 adaptable			
2 creative			
3 hard-working			
4 motivated			
5 able to work on own			
6 dogged			
7 supported (by family, etc.)			
8 ready to do mundane jobs			
9 able to overcome setbacks			
10 have common sense			

If you answer mostly 'No' or have ticked more than half of the 'Could become', then perhaps you should question whether you are ready to start a business or work on your own. A few 'Could become' ticks suggests motivation, too many suggests not being prepared.

Test

(See page 197 for answers.)

1 Describe a business plan in one sentence.
2 Name two types of plan.
3 Name three reasons for writing a business plan.
4 What are the areas usually covered by a plan?
5 Name one thing a business plan cannot do.
6 Who is the best person to write your plan?

Summary

A business plan is an important business tool. It is a guide for future action as well as a means of showing potential backers that your business is viable. Whether you write the plan alone or with colleagues it needs to be created with the intended audience in mind. Before you begin, work out what skills you or your colleagues will need so that you are aware of any potential gaps in the plan.

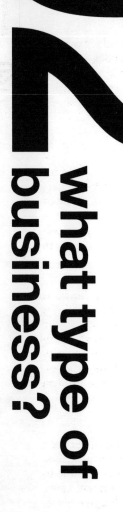

02 what type of business?

In this chapter you will learn:

- how to choose a legal identity
- how to protect your business idea
- how to focus your business idea
- how to test your business idea

You need to be clear about the type of business you want. You must decide whether you are providing a product or service, or both. You need to describe your business in your plan. There is a legal form to a business too. The legal implications depend on what form your business takes. These will affect your liabilities and how the business is run.

The legal side

In your business plan you will need to provide details about the legal ownership of your business. Any potential lender, investor, grant provider or anyone who might offer other kinds of help will want to know that you have the legal right to be negotiating with them and that your business is, or will be, created in accordance with the correct legal procedures.

Types of business ownership

There are several kinds of business ownership and each has its benefits and problems:

- sole trader
- partnership
- limited company

Sole trader

This is a common type of small business ownership. The business is owned and operated by one individual. If you run a business on these lines you get all the profits and are liable for all the debts. Your trading name and address must appear on all documents. You need to tell the Inland Revenue and Social Security the date that you started working for yourself and the date you actually started trading. You do not, however, have to publish your accounts.

Partnership

Two or more individuals together form a partnership of between two and 20 members. Each partner has a liability for all debts. You don't have to have a contract drawn up but it is sensible to ensure that you have an agreement about issues that might cause conflict, such as what happens if all the partners disagree on an issue, how much investment each partner must make in the business and what is the procedure to be followed if one partner wants to leave the business. A solicitor can advise you of the best means of doing this. Partners can be active or sleeping. Sleeping partners invest in the business but do not take part in its day-to-day running. They are only liable for the amount of their initial investment. At least one partner must be a general partner with unlimited liability for all the debts of the partnership.

Limited company

This is a difficult business type to set up. Once a limited company has been set up it becomes a legal entity entirely separate from whoever owns it. The individuals who own it are not liable for anything except the shares that they have. The company must pay corporation tax on any profits and PAYE and National Insurance for its employees. Directors and employees must pay class one insurance and have National Insurance and tax deducted from their salaries. Limited companies can be public or private. This is a decision your accountant can help you make depending on the type of business you have.

BUSINESS PLAN TIP

Talk to people who run different types of businesses before deciding which type of legal format and operation would suit you. Ask them to be honest about the drawbacks as well as the benefits.

Other business types

There are other types of businesses that you might want to consider.

Consultancy

This is a business where you are offering your service to others as an expert in your field. It can be run by one person (the consultant) or can be a business in which more than one consultant is available to provide the service. (The business plan for Acme Consulting at the back of this book is an example of this type of business.)

Co-operative

When many people band together to operate a business on an equal footing, it is known as a co-operative. Everyone puts the same amount of time and money into the business, works and reaps the benefit equally.

Franchise

A franchise is a popular way of starting in a business. You buy the rights to trade under the parent company name and in return get a business already run on a proven successful idea. You pay the franchiser a royalty fee based on your sales. Although nearly three-quarters of all new businesses fail, most franchises are successful. Most franchisers provide training, advice and, where applicable, contacts as well as supplying the basic stock.

Choosing a trading name

If you are a sole trader you may want to trade under your own name. If you want to use a trade name and perhaps a logo you should apply to register the design of the logo as a trademark and check that the name you want to use is not controlled. If, as a sole trader, you want to trade under another name you must still ensure that your own name appears on all documents related to your business sent out to the public.

Registering a company name

If you decide to set up a limited company, you will need to register it at Companies House. You will need to provide Companies House, and the people you deal with, with certain information for the record. There are four main types of company:

- private, limited by shares
- private, limited by guarantee
- private unlimited
- public limited company (PLC)

For the purposes of this book the private limited company is likely to be the one kind you might consider at the moment. You need to provide a memorandum of association detailing the company name, the address of the registered office and what it will do. You also need to provide articles of association which set out the rules for how the company's internal affairs will be run. A private company must have at least one director and one secretary and must make annual accounts available. For further information look at the Companies House website (see Taking it Further).

Protecting your idea

Depending on what kinds of products or services your business will be dealing with, you will probably want to know how you can protect your trading name, logo, designs or creative work. Protecting your original ideas will be important to you, and the business should be protected against copying or 'passing off'. There are several ways you can do this:

- registering a patent
- registering a trade mark
- registering a design
- protecting copyright

Detailed information about all these means of protection can be found at the website of the UK Patent Office (see Taking it Further).

Registering a patent

A patent is granted by the government to an inventor and protects how your idea works. It gives you ownership of the invention and the right to prevent other people from making, using or selling it. If you have invented the better mousetrap (and many people think they have) you need to protect it from exploitation by others by applying for a patent from the UK Patent Office. Applying for a patent is not straightforward. You have to supply several detailed documents and you might want to employ a patent procurer to ensure that your application is completed correctly.

Registering a trademark

Your trademark is a sign that distinguishes your products and services from anyone else's. It might include any combination of words, symbols or pictures. Even if you have registered your business name at Companies House, it does not mean that your trademark is also protected so you need to register your trademark separately.

Registering a design

If you have created a product that has a new and individual character in either its form or decoration then you might be able to register it. This can be done through The UK Patent Office (details in Taking it Further).

Protecting copyright

If your business will involve producing original writing, artwork or other creative work then your work is automatically protected in the UK. Musical, dramatic, literary or artistic work is protected for 70 years after the death of the author. You do not need to use a copyright symbol. Although your copyright will probably be protected in most places abroad, this is not invariably so. There is no way of proving originality of your work except by arguing it in court in the case of supposed infringement of copyright. Some people deposit a copy of their work in a bank or with a solicitor. However, if you think your copyright is infringed, bear in mind legal costs. It might well be quicker and cheaper to sort out the problem with the infringer.

Products or services?

You need to work out early on whether you will be providing products or services and whether you will be selling them directly to your customers or indirectly. Generally you can divide these into several types:

- product sold directly to customer (e.g. in shops)
- products sold indirectly to customer (e.g. to wholesaler)
- services with personal customer contact (e.g. alternative healer)
- services with distant contact with customers (e.g. telephone secretarial services)

Until you know what kind of service or product you will offer you will not be able to write your business plan.

You no doubt already have your business idea. Now is the time to think about exactly what kind of business you will be running. Will it require employees, retail outlets, a mail order service, a website? Or perhaps you intend to offer a service in people's homes or do everything for your customers yourself in your own home?

Your business idea

Your business idea should be so clear in your mind that you can describe it in one or two sentences. Ask yourself, 'What is my business for? What exactly will it do?' The answer to these questions will form the basis of your plan. For example, your business might 'provide healthy, home-made packed lunches for pre-school children delivered to homes on a daily basis', or 'create and sell high-quality hand-decorated pens through a website and in high street stores.'

The main business idea that you put in your business plan should be related to the type of business that you have or intend to have. You need to describe how the business is or will be set up and its main purpose. To do this you need to explain its key objectives.

The two-minute lift rule

Here is a tip to help you focus your business idea. Imagine you are in a lift with a millionaire who promises to invest in your business if you can explain your idea convincingly in the time it takes to get to the right floor – two minutes. So two minutes is all the time you have to say what your product or service is and what is important about it. Not long. If you want that money you have to be able to pitch your idea in one or two sharply focused sentences. Try it.

Focusing on key objectives

Closely associated with your main business idea is the need to focus on the key objectives of your business and how you see your business idea fitting in with them. In your plan you need to focus on the key objectives, that is the main aims for your business. Ask yourself:

- what do I want the business to achieve?
- what are my goals for the business?
- how will my business idea contribute to the main goals of my business?

When you have the answers to these questions you will be better prepared to focus your research for your business idea. A plan that can demonstrate clearly a well thought-out and focused business idea that fits in with the main aims of the business has a better chance of success.

The key goals of your business will be closely related to why you want to establish the business (apart from the money). Is it fame, a chance to change the world, to be the best in the business? Whatever it is it, you need to make sure that you are clear about your business aims and where your idea fits in with it.

Is your idea SMART?

One way of testing your business idea is to use the SMART test. This will help you discover whether your idea is achievable. SMART encourages you to ask questions about your idea. Get your SMART answers right and you will be well on the way to creating a realistic plan. So SMART asks, is the idea:

S   Specific?
M   Measurable?
A   Attainable?
R   Realistic?
T   Timely?

Specific

Can you precisely describe your business idea? Saying vaguely that you'd 'quite like to sell cars' isn't an idea. You need to be precise: 'I want to buy second-hand cars, restore them and repaint them with modern art and sell them to inner-city high-fliers'. The more precisely you can define the idea and explain what you want to do and who you want to sell to, the more chance it has of being realized.

Measurable

How will you decide when your plan is successful? Will it be by the number of products sold? The number of customers your service caters for? The number of countries that you sell to? The number of outlets you create? You need to decide how to measure success.

Attainable

Can you achieve your goals? How long are you allowing to attain success with your plan? If you underestimate your resources or the timescale or your personnel, your plan may not develop as it should. Make sure that your goals are clear and that you have a precise strategy for achieving them. If you have decided upon an unrealistic timescale ('I will get the business up and running in a month') or only employ three people to do the job of 25, for example, then your idea is unattainable.

Realistic

This is the 'selling snow to Greenland' problem. Your plan has to be realistic. If you try to sell the wrong product or service to potential customers, or simply do not have the skills or the management team to make the plan work then it won't succeed.

There might be practical problems that make it impossible to work. For example, you might want to sell worldwide when you can realistically only manage to cater for a small local population, or you are relying on family support and help when they have other plans for their lives. Think carefully about whether your idea has a realistic chance of working.

Timely

Don't underestimate the importance of timing in getting your plan to succeed. 'An idea whose time has come' is not a joke – if your brilliant idea hits an astonished world too early or too late, it won't work. If competitors have got there first or you haven't done any market research and therefore don't realize that potential customers simply won't be interested in what you want to sell, then your timing is wrong. Being timely also means that, assuming you are convinced that what you sell will be welcomed by customers, you can get it into the market place at an optimal time.

Improving on SMART

Your answers to the SMART test might show that you are not quite ready to put your plan into operation. But it also gives you the chance to improve your idea. For example, if your plan is unrealistic you can plan ways to alter it to become more possible. Or if you realize that you have not got a way of measuring your success, it is something that can be remedied. By getting the SMART answers correct now, you can present a business plan that has a good chance of success.

Questionnaire
1 Have you chosen a trading name?
2 Do you need to register a design or logo or apply for a patent?
3 What kind of business do you want to form?
4 Will you offer a product, service or both?
5 Do you intend to employ other people?
6 Do you need to get advice from professionals about any of the above?

Can you afford it?

Before you take the next step and go ahead with your business idea you need to consider whether you can afford to take the financial risks necessary to get started. Unless you have enough capital of your own to proceed, you will have to approach lenders or investors and this will involve putting up security. You need to decide whether you can afford to do this.

Security

To raise money from a long-term lender or venture capitalists you will need to put up security. This might take one or more of several forms:

- personal savings
- equity on your home
- endowment policies or life insurance

You need to decide whether your business will be sound enough to take the risk of putting up your home as security. If you have a family it is something you need to discuss with your partner. After all, if the business fails and you lose the property, so does your family.

Investors of capital will want something from a business such as limited control of it or a percentage of the profits equal to a percentage of ownership. Before they will consider investing their money they will want to be convinced that the business is or will be financially viable and likely to provide them with a reasonable return on their investment. They will also require a get-out clause so that they can withdraw if the business fails, or looks like failing.

You might be able to arrange an initial loan by means of equity capital without interest and agree that it will be repaid when the business is a success. It is not a good idea to get a bank loan to do this because a bank might decide to recall the loan before you are ready to do so.

The type of finance you want will affect the sources of finance you approach. For example, if you want a short-term loan you can approach banks; if you want venture capital you might be better off approaching business contacts or the Enterprise Investment Scheme (see Taking if Further).

Test
(See page 197 for answers.)
1 Name three kinds of business ownership.
2 Name one other kind of business type.

3 Where would you register a company name?
4 Where would you register a design?
5 How long does the copyright on creative work generally last?
6 What does the acronym SMART stand for?
7 What do investors need from you?

Plan preparation

Write one or two paragraphs describing the main business idea that you are presenting in your plan (use the two-minute lift rule described earlier in this chapter to focus it). Include the results of the SMART analysis and explain how the idea would contribute to the main aims of your business. Be as precise as possible. Write a paragraph explaining why your business was or will be established and how your business idea will contribute to this. Think about the following points:

1 Decide whether you are offering a product or a service.
2 Decide what type of business you want to run.
3 Choose a legal framework for the business.
4 Look at the Companies House website to see what steps you need to take to register your company, if relevant.
5 If you have patent or trademark issues, read the UK Patent Office website for instructions about how to proceed.
6 Write a sentence describing your main business idea as modified by any SMART analysis.
7 Check what security you can offer.

Summary

You need to be clear about whether you are offering a product or service and what kind of legal format your business will take. You also need to decide whether you need to deal with such things as registering a trademark, taking out a patent or safeguarding copyright. Consider whether other types of business set-up such as a consultancy or franchise might be a more suitable way of operating your business. Test your business idea the SMART way to decide whether your idea is viable. Ensure that you are clear about your main business idea and that you can put up any financial security required by lenders or investors.

03 what are you selling?

In this chapter you will learn:

- how to decide what you are selling
- how to decide where and what to sell
- how to focus on the benefits
- how to ensure you sell what people want
- how to analyse saleability

A description of what you intend to sell is one of the most important parts of your business plan. You need to provide a clear explanation of what service or product you will be selling and what it does or how you will operate it. By setting this out in writing you will be able to see whether your idea is fully developed and ready to put into the marketplace. You may be supplying both products and services, in which case you will need to explain how you will integrate them.

Anyone reading your business plan will want to see the answer to some basic questions:

- are you selling a product or service?
- where are you going to sell it?
- how is your product or service different from everyone else's?
- how will your product or service benefit customers?
- is there a demand for what you are selling?
- what kind of image do you want your product or service to project?
- will you make your product or supply the service yourself, or will you buy in the product and employ others to provide the service?
- how will you distribute it?
- how much will it cost you to create the product or service you supply?
- how much will you charge your customers?

The answers to these questions will ensure that you can convince readers of your plan, and that you understand what you are selling and what a viable price would be.

Sales targets

Your ultimate aim is to achieve revenue from sales. To do that you need to set targets and objectives for your sales. For a new business these targets will be presented in the form of sales forecasts. You will need to set out the sales forecasts according to different types of products or services (if more than one), by volume and value (if relevant), by sales into different types of customers (local/national, male/female or other groups relevant to your business) and sales by different distribution methods (e.g. post, retail stores, house-to-house sales). More information about writing the sales forecasts is given in Chapter 8.

Product or service?

As mentioned in the previous chapter, if you have not already done so you might need to decide whether you are providing a product or service. Although we think these are easily distinguished from each other, sometimes it can be difficult to decide which definition fits what you are selling. For example, a book is a product. If you publish the book you are selling a product; if you hunt for out-of-date books for customers you are providing a book-search service. If you publish your own books and sell them at talks you give then you are providing a product (the book) and a service (the talk). The key question you should ask is:

What am I getting paid for?

Define this first to decide what your actual product or service is. Write down exactly what you are providing, for example, I will be supplying customers with a fast, cheap book-finding service. To further define what you are selling, ask yourself the following questions:

- how do I describe what I am selling to my customers?
- am I providing something that is the result of having created something, or am I doing something for somebody else?
- am I supplying a product and service? If so, am I providing them separately or as part of a package?

Remember that in business terms a product can be touched. In non-business terms a product might simply be something you have created but which cannot be touched, such as the performance of a play. In business terms the performance of a play would be a service, the printed copy of the play a product.

If you are intending to sell a range of products or services you need to be able to describe the different components of the range and how they relate to each other.

Where will you sell it?

The next thing anyone reading your business plan will want to know is where you are going to sell your product or service. This will be referred to again in more detail in Chapter 5, but for the purposes of defining your product you need to know whether you will be selling it:

- yourself
- through others

- directly to the customer from your own workplace or home
- to the customer through a retail outlet
- by mail or internet

Where you intend to sell will limit the type of service or product you can offer. You will not, for example, be able to provide ice creams directly to customers from your home if you have not got the facilities or space to make the ice cream and store it.

Selling it yourself

If you have a product or service that is easy to store and you can sell directly to the public you might want to sell it yourself. You need to bear in mind that if you are doing the selling, then you will have less time for running the business. This might be fine if you are, for example, an artist selling your own paintings, but not so practical if you offer a cleaning service. In the latter case, it might be more practical to employ someone to do the cleaning and run the office.

Employing others to sell it

If you will not have the time to both run and create or provide your service or product you will need to employ others to do the selling for you. This puts you at one remove from your customers and brings into question all kinds of legal and practical obligations to your employee. Readers of your business plan will want to know why you have chosen one method of selling.

Selling from home

You need to be able to explain where you will sell your product or service. Will you be selling it from home? In which case, will you be sending a product out or selling it on the premises? Will you be providing a service where customers visit your home, or one where they will contact you at home although you never meet?

BUSINESS PLAN TIP

Before deciding whether to run your business from home, ask your family whether they would be happy about it. They might be willing to tolerate it or get involved, or they might be unhappy about the amount of time you have to devote to it. It might be better for family harmony to work elsewhere if they are likely to object!

Selling through others

You might employ other people to sell for you. They might work directly from their homes or your workplace or go out to customers. Or they might sell for you in a retail outlet. If you will be employing other people to do the selling you will need to think about:

- training – they need to know what they are selling as well as you do
- trust – how will you ensure that you employ trustworthy people?
- pay – can you afford to employ other people?
- legal and financial obligations, e.g. tax, insurance, sick pay, health and safety

Selling through space

You may decide to sell by providing your product or service by mail or on the internet. In this way you do not meet your customers, but you may have to consider things such as storage, insurance and credit card safety. However you will be selling, you need to be able to explain the method clearly.

What is your USP?

Everything you sell should have a USP – a Unique Selling Point. That is the one thing that will make your customers buy what you are selling, and buy it from *you*. It is important that you know what makes your product or service different from everyone else's. What makes it original? This doesn't mean that it has to be necessarily completely different from what other people sell, but it should offer something original in the way of benefit to the customer, otherwise why would anyone buy it in preference to others? Think carefully about how what you will sell is different. Consider the following areas:

- price (e.g. cheaper)
- improved version (e.g. more efficient, faster)
- method of delivery (e.g. faster, more reliable)
- looks (e.g. more up-to-date)
- where sold (e.g. by mail rather than on the doorstep)
- originality (e.g. completely new – nobody else sells it)
- geography (e.g. available in a new part of the country)

- service – (e.g. how you sell is better)
- fashion (e.g. there are others, but yours is this year's 'in' colour)

Of course, there are many more ways in which you could provide a USP, but you must have one. Nobody will put money into helping you produce and sell a mousetrap unless you can convince them that it has a USP that will make customers buy it rather than the ones already on sale (it comes with its own irresistible-to-mice cheese?).

Benefits to others

Nobody will buy what you sell unless it has some benefit for them. This is a key point that must be included in your business plan. You may have found a USP but it may not be something that customers want. What you sell must provide one or more benefits for your customers. Your USP might be a benefit, but not necessarily. If you sell milk in orange bottles it will be different, but how does it benefit the customer? If you explain that it will make it easier to find in a large fridge, they might be tempted (but perhaps not). You need to explain what your customer will get out of what you sell. Bear in mind too that not all benefits are tangible. You will not only be selling a product or service but also aspirations. Consider whether what you sell will, for example, improve people's lifestyles, give them an advantage at work, demonstrate their financial status or show them to be part of an up-to-date trend. What you sell should make people feel good about themselves. Will it help them:

- do something better, more easily, faster?
- look or feel better?
- gain an advantage over other people?
- save money, space, anxiety?
- be happier, richer, better looking?
- own something they desire?

What benefits will you provide?

BUSINESS PLAN TIP
Use a spider diagram to help you work out your business idea and how it benefits customers (see Figure 1).

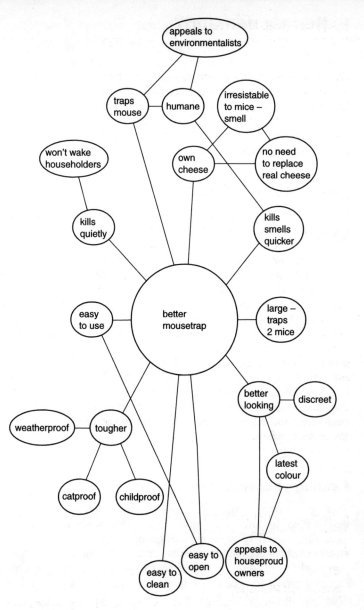

Figure 1: example spider diagram

Is there a demand?

This will be covered more fully in Chapter 4 where we will discuss how to do basic market research. Here you need to think about whether anyone will really want what you sell. It is no good having a brilliant idea but being unable to sell the result because there is no demand for it. To find out who your customers will be you will need to do some basic research. You will also need to back up this research with facts and figures. In your business plan it will be no good writing that you talked to your friends and lots of people thought it was a good idea. How many people in your area want it? Would they buy it if you provided it? How would they want to get it?

What image will you project?

The image your product or service projects is part of what will sell it. Readers of your business plan will want to discover whether you are aware of that image and how you will ensure that it will be suitable for your customers. The image can be the result of many things such as status, utility or aspirations. For example, if what you sell will be something that makes people feel part of a select or popular group, then you are selling status. If you are selling something that everyone feels to be necessary because of its usefulness, then you are selling utility. It is no good selling something useful that customers perceive to be shameful to possess or use. Remember the jokes about a certain kind of car? The car was perfectly good but in the public's mind it had an image of being an embarrassment to drive. It took hard work and a lot of money for the company to overcome the wrong kind of image.

Finding your niche

Part of the image your product or service will project will be determined by the niche into which you wish to fit it. For example, to sell to a particular group of people you need to ensure that the image fits with what they will find desirable. So you might wish to sell to the 13 to 18 year age group and would therefore want to project an image that would be exciting, fashionable, cheap and instantly available.

How to discover who will buy from you is explored in Chapter 5, but all this is information that needs to go into your business plan.

Make a list

Sit down and make a list of the niche or niches you want to sell to, and then work out what image you want to evoke. Ask these questions about your niche:

1 Exactly who do I want to sell to?
2 Where do they live?
3 What do they like doing?
4 What do they aspire to?
5 Who do they associate with?

Then ask these questions about image:

1 Will my product or service look right?
2 Will its image represent the right benefit (e.g. utility, price, status)?
3 Is the image suitable for my intended customers?
4 Will the image be short- or long-term?
5 Will the image be adaptable?

Remember that you are not only selling the product or service itself but a lifestyle choice.

Make it yourself?

For any creative person starting a business this question might seem unnecessary. You will create your own product and probably sell it yourself. But even for such people there might well come a time when the question becomes relevant. If you start by making the product or providing the service yourself, you have complete control over the production process, everything from the design to the packaging. This is really only possible if you only ever intend to sell a very limited number of products or provide a service well within your personal limits of delivery. Once you intend to produce or provide more than you can deliver personally, you will need to employ other people. The decision on whether to stay small and work alone or expand and employ other people is one that successful small businesses have to make eventually.

Once you employ other people to make your product you are probably at the stage when you will need to employ other people to sell it as well. Once you do that you have the problems that come with employing others and you are once again at one or more removes from what you are selling.

There are benefits of making or selling the product yourself if possible:

- you control the process from start to finish
- you control the image
- you have a one-to-one relationship with the customer
- you can plan the future of your business without any interference

What you sell is tied in with how you sell. If you want to sell a product yourself but intend to sell to a great many people then you might have to employ other people. If you want to sell to a lot of people but can only provide one daily service call then you will have to employ others or alter your expectations.

How will you distribute?

This will be discussed in more detail in Chapter 7. Here we can say that distribution is tied to what you can sell. If you want to operate by sending a product by ordinary post you can't sell a massage service or sell very bulky products (unless you use a different kind of postal service). You will be limited to such things as books, slim boxes, small products, etc. On the other hand the product or service might dictate the method of distribution. So selling made-to-measure shoes might mean that you can only do so by personal contact with the customer. Or selling computers to foreign countries might mean that you have to do so through a third party.

Production costs

What you sell might also be determined by how much it will cost you to create the product or start the service. If these costs are too high you have some alternatives:

- ask for more money in the form of loans or investments or grants
- change the product or service
- change the way you sell

How much will you charge?

The price of what you sell is important in the scheme of things. What you sell might be determined by its possible selling price. If you want to raise a lot of money quickly then you might consider selling something that is already poplar or has wide appeal.

If you want to enter a niche market then you might be able to do so by selling at a higher price because of the scarcity value. (Pricing is discussed in more detail in Chapter 8.)

SWOT analysis

This concept of analysing a problem will be introduced in other chapters as it has many relevancies. Here it is intended to help you examine what makes your product saleable and how you will relate to the competition.

Analysis using the **SWOT** list:
- Strengths
- Weaknesses
- Opportunities
- Threats

Strengths

What are the benefits of your product or service? What benefits does the competition offer? Why and how does your product offer better or more benefits than theirs?

Weaknesses

What weaknesses can you find? Does the competition have the same or different weaknesses? Can you turn the weaknesses into benefits or strengths? How can you reduce the weaknesses or eliminate them?

Opportunities

Is there an obvious gap in the market? Are any of your competitors aiming to fill that gap? How can you adapt what you sell to make the most of the opportunities?

Threats

Where are the threats coming from? Are they coming from competitors, economic climate, government regulations, changing public perceptions and needs? How can you turn threats into strengths or opportunities?

Facing the competition

In your business plan you will need to demonstrate that you know exactly who or what your competition is and how you are going to deal with it. If you cannot demonstrate that you have a good understanding of the competition and how you will deal with it, investors will not have the confidence in your business that they need. In your plan you need to be able to describe the competition that your product or service faces and what its strengths and weaknesses are. There is more in Chapter 7 about how to analyse the competition.

Buying and developing

It will not be enough to say in your plan that you have a good product or service and that you can sell it. Readers of your plan will want to know how you will obtain what you sell and how you will develop it.

Buying the product

Buying the product or paying for setting up your service is an important factor of starting a business or operating an existing one. The cost might determine what you sell. If you cannot afford it, then you might have to change what you sell or how you sell it or raise money to do so.

Developing the product

It is rare that a product or service will not need developing or changing in the future. This might be to adapt to new trends and customer needs, to improve the product or service, or to comply with new regulations or delivery changes. The costs of doing this must be estimated and included in your plan.

The pros and cons of your product or service

You need to include a summary paragraph in your plan explaining the pros and cons of your product or service after you are clear about what you are offering customers and what the competition is.

Ten questions you must answer

1 What *exactly* am I selling?
2 What are its benefits?

3 What is its USP?
4 What does its SWOT analysis show?
5 Will it have a long- or short-term life?
6 Who or what is the competition?
7 In what ways is their product better or worse than mine?
8 Can I compete successfully?
9 Will the costs of production limit what I can sell?
10 How often and in what ways will the product or service need
   to be developed?

Test
(See page 197 for answers.)
1 What does USP mean?
2 Name one way to work out your business's USP.
3 What type of analysis can tell you how your product or service
   relates to the competition?
4 Name two benefits of making or selling the product or service
   yourself.

Plan preparation

Decide exactly what you are selling and write a description of
your product or service. Explain how it will benefit your customers and in which ways it will differ from the competition.
Emphasize its USP. If it is part of a range, explain how the components relate to each other. Include the results of your SWOT
analysis and explain how you would overcome any weaknesses.
Briefly mention proposed methods of supply and distribution
and make rough costs for these. These will be expanded on in
Chapters 7 and 8 when operations and finances will be discussed.

Summary

You cannot successfully sell anything nor convince investors of the
business's viability unless you are clear about exactly what your
product or service is. To do this you need to understand its benefits
and USP. Use a SWOT analysis to assess it. You also need to research
and assess the competition. Remember that production costs might
determine what you sell. You also need to decide how much and in
what way development will take place and the likely costs.

04 who are your customers?

In this chapter you will learn:

- how to decide who your customers are
- what market research can do
- basic market research techniques
- how to promote customer satisfaction
- how to calculate total demand

Your business plan will need to contain a clear statement of who your customers are and where you expect to find them. Before you can write this section of the plan you need to have done a lot of research about your customers. The more research you can do, the better your plan will be; however, even basic information can be valuable.

What kinds of customers?

Your customers can cover a wide range of people. Don't forget that they might include organizations as well as individuals. Make a list of your potential customers and see whether they include:

- individuals
- groups, e.g. co-ops
- organizations, e.g. charities
- corporate bodies

Unless you are dealing with individual customers you will be selling to people within an organization, large or small. These people fall under the main headings of:

- buyers
- decision-makers

Your approach to these various kinds of customer will vary according to their role within the organization. What you sell must appeal to them as representatives of their organization.

You also need to take into account the concerns of people who help you get your product to customers, such as:

- distributors
- suppliers
- agents
- wholesalers
- individuals in organizations you deal with

The product or service must not only appeal to customers but must satisfy criteria that concern these people or they will not deal with you. An example of this is the agency that will not ask its reps to sell a book because it does not satisfy criteria that will make it sell, such as a striking cover. When you are deciding what to sell you need to take all these things into account.

Why do you need customer information?

You cannot target your customers effectively unless you know a great deal of information about them. Anyone reading your plan needs to know that you know precisely who your customers are and where to find them. Any marketing you do will be far less effective if you are simply telling everyone that your product is available and hoping that the people who will be really interested will find it.

Aims of market research

You will need to use market research to find out about your customers. The aims of market research are to provide people running a business with the information they need to make informed decisions. Market research involves gathering, analysing, interpreting and presenting data in an organized way. It can then be used to help inform market decisions. You can do basic market research yourself but can also employ a market researcher or market research agency. As we shall see later in this book, you will need to do some market research to find out about your competitors as well as your customers.

Information about your customers will help you target them and convince readers of your business plan that you know what you are doing. After all, you need to know who your customers are so that you can sell to them and continue to sell to them. Knowing your target customers convinces readers that your business has a viable future. You will need to know at least something about the following:

- geography – e.g. where do your customers live?
- age – e.g. children between the ages of 3 and 10, adults over 18
- sex – is your product or service suitable for only one sex or both (be careful here; just because it might be suitable for one sex does not mean you should refuse to sell it to the other)
- education – would your product or service appeal to customers with a particular level of education, e.g. higher, primary school age
- residence – the kind of dwellings your customers live in, e.g. flat, mansion, council house
- likes and dislikes – e.g. do they like pop music and restaurants or are you more likely to find them listening to jazz or climbing mountains?

- disposable income – can your customers afford what you sell?
- jobs – e.g. are you more likely to sell to office workers or home workers?
- family – e.g. are your customers likely to be single and living on their own or part of an extended family?
- how they prefer to receive your product – e.g. from shops, by mail, from doorstep salespeople?
- when and how often your customers will buy?
- why will customers buy what you sell and why will they buy it from you?

These are just a few of the basic questions you should ask; obviously, there are many more. You will also be able to think of questions specific to your type of business. The more details you have about your customers, the better you can target your product or service to their needs and target any marketing to reach them.

Geography

Where your customers live is obviously very important. If you supply a product you might be able to sell it over a much wider area than a service, particularly if the service is geared towards particular local needs. You need to think about:

- how you will get to your customers (car, public transport, foot)
- how you will get the product or service to them (mail, internet, shops, personal collection, doorstep salespeople)
- whether you intend to sell outside your own country (think about export rules, customs, cost, etc.)

When you have answered these questions you might find that your options are circumscribed by practical considerations.

Age

An obvious piece of information you need about your customers is their age. Some products or services will be uniquely suitable for certain age groups, for example rattles for a baby, alcoholic drinks for over-18s, pensions for working age adults. Others might cross age barriers, for example trainer shoes, jeans, food, holidays. If what you sell is to do well then it must be targeted at the correct age range and readers will expect to see knowledge of this in your plan.

Sex

This needs careful thought. Is your product or service suitable for only men or only women? Nowadays, and bearing in mind sex discrimination laws, there will be virtually nothing that either sex might not find desirable, but there will be things that one sex might prefer to another. Although you should be happy to sell to whoever wants it (except in the case of things deemed lawfully unsuitable for anyone under-age) you might want to target one sex or another. Women's magazines, for example, are bought by men as well as women but are targeted at women. Whatever you decide, you must be able to justify it in your plan.

Education

What you sell might be more appealing to people who have a certain level or type of education. For example, you might assume (perhaps erroneously) that classical records are more likely to be bought by people who have been through higher education. Or you might be producing an educational toy that would appeal mainly to primary school children (or their parents).

Residence

The type of property your customers are likely to live in might also have a bearing on the type of service or product you offer or to whom you direct it. This might be because it is directly related to the type of building or because customers will be buying into aspirations to create a certain type of residence (for example, town dwellers wanting to recreate the rustic look). Or you might make assumptions about the type of people who live in certain kinds of property.

When and how often customers buy

This is important to find out because it will affect how you run your business. This needs to be made explicit in your plan. What you sell might be seasonal or affected by other influences. Your customers might buy a product or service frequently because they consider it essential or it might be an occasional luxury or emergency purchase. Knowledge of your customers' buying habits is vital to ensuring that your product or service is available at the right time or in the right quantities.

Why buy it?

It is also important to find out why customers buy the product or service. Is it something that everyone in their peer group buys?

Have they been affected by advertisements? Do they like the colour, shape, price? If you are going to sell to them you need to know what will attract them to what you sell.

Likes and dislikes

It might seem odd to try to discover what your customers like but it is an important part of understanding them and whether they would be receptive to what you sell. Companies frequently go to great lengths to try to discover their customers' hobbies, shopping preferences, possessions and so on because it provides a more detailed picture of their clients. This will be discussed in more detail later, but if you know, for example, that your customers will be single women between the ages of 35 and 55 who like rock music and walking, you might well sell them fashionable walking boots but fail to sell them classical CDs.

Why these customers?

In your plan it will be no good just recording the answers to the questions above. You need to be able to explain why you have chosen to sell to these particular customers. Is it because they all live locally to you? Perhaps they have been asking for a service like yours for years? Is your product or service particularly suited to a certain group of people?

For some businesses your customer base will be obvious – if you sell a coat for rabbits you will be selling to pet owners, for example. If you sell something that could appeal to a wide range of customers your customer base might not be so obvious. Think in terms of segmentation, that is positioning your product or service to particular sections of the population. If you divide your customers into groups you can tailor what you sell and how you sell it to each group. The segments need to be large enough to be profitable but measurable so that you can tell whether you have reached your target customers.

Segmentation

You might segment your customers into groups based on broad terms such as their attitudes, employment or income. Or perhaps by location, type of buyer, type of dwelling or family type. If you sell to industry you could segment by industrial sector, number of employees or country. So one business might target mothers under 30 living in south-east England who work outside the home and earn less than £15,000. Another might aim at biscuit-makers in Eastern Europe with 10 to 60 employees.

Customers as organizations

Customers can be organizations as well as individuals. Although it is the organizations themselves that you have to sell to, you will be pitching towards the individuals in organizations who have the power to buy. Your product or service must be what is required by them and they will have their own likes and dislikes.

Your first task will be to find out what the organization needs. Then find out who in the organization makes decisions about buying, who has the spending power, who decides what features a product or service needs. You need to find out what their spending limits are and how they make their purchasing decisions. You might have to be on their list of approved suppliers and, if so, you need to find out how to get on it. Once on it, will you be automatically invited to bid? Who do you need to keep in contact with?

How to reach your customers

You need to find out how your customers prefer to receive what you sell. If they prefer to buy by mail they may be put off by a product or service that can only be obtained from a shop. Knowing this will not only help you reach your customers more effectively but also determine your distribution costs.

You need to define the area you intend to deliver to and sell in. In broad terms this could be:

- local
- national
- international
- worldwide

Don't overestimate your capabilities with delivery but be prepared to expand if your business does well.

How to find out about your customers

It is all very well saying that you need to know who your customers are, but how do you find out the basic information about them? This is part of the job of market research. This is not the

place to give detailed instructions on how to go about creating
and carrying out a market research project; there are many good
books available (see Taking it Further). However, a brief explanation of what sources you can use follows.

There are two main types of research:

* field research – collecting raw data from people
* desk research – finding information in published works

Desk research is done by using published works, phone calls and
the internet to get information. Field research involves getting
original data from individuals. Some methods for obtaining original data from your customers fall into a few categories:

* interviews
* questionnaires
* observation
* hall tests
* market testing

Interviews

The best way to find out what your potential customers want is
simply to ask them. This can be done by conducting interviews
with them yourself or by employing other people to do so. The
interviews might be conducted one-to-one or in focus groups.
Either way, you need to decide what questions you will ask by
deciding what you want to know. Even if you decide that an
informal discussion would be more useful, you still need to know
what questions you want answers to and so be able to guide the
discussion.

Pros

Interviews have the advantage that you are asking people directly
and can immediately add or subtract questions as necessary. You
get the answers quickly.

Cons

Some people may be shy about speaking to somebody in
person. If you are doing door-to-door interviews your subjects
may not be available. If you are conducting street interviews
you may not be able to stop enough people of your customer
target profile. If you are conducting the interviews yourself you
might not have the time or energy to interview as many people
as necessary.

Questionnaires

This is a popular method of discovering customers' likes and dislikes. A carefully constructed questionnaire will contain specially chosen questions which are relevant but unbiased and which allow the recipients time to answer them. They can be handed out in the street to likely targets, posted, put on the internet, e-mailed or kept at a stall. If you provide a space for 'further comments' you can broaden the questionnaire's usefulness.

You should not need to ask for respondents' names and contact details. If you do need to do so, ensure that their rights under the Data Protection Act are maintained (see Taking it Further for contact details of the Information Commissioner's Office).

Pros

You can reach a larger target base and ensure that everybody receives the same questions. You might get a higher response if your targets prefer written to oral communication or who prefer to answer questions in their own time, perhaps, busy mothers or academics.

Cons

Questionnaires can get ignored or only partially completed. If the questions are not clear enough recipients may respond to the wrong questions. Some questionnaires may get thrown away. Response time might be slower if recipients delay sending the form back. You need to factor in costs for postage and printing.

Observation

If you sell a product you can go to the point of sale and watch what customers look at, what they buy, what they ask for. Or, if possible, go to places where they use the product and see what problems they have and how they use it. If you sell a service, accompany a service provider on some visits to customers to assess their satisfaction and see any practical problems for yourself.

Pros

You can see what customers really do and get first-hand knowledge of their buying preferences and habits.

Cons

If you are seen it might affect customer behaviour. You can only form judgements about what you actually see; customers might exhibit other behaviour out of your sight.

Hall tests

In this research method selected people are invited to a nearby hall or large room close to a shopping centre. They are asked to evaluate products and are interviewed about them. The tests might take place in several different towns to achieve a larger sample.

Pros

These tests provide immediate feedback on the product itself and can be used to evaluate a wide range of other things such as advertising, price, product name and packaging.

Cons

It can be expensive to hire a hall and the necessary staff as well as providing incentives to people taking part. There is always the danger that interviewees will say what they think the interviewer wants to hear.

Testing the market

You could try selling your product or service in a limited area for a limited time to see customers' reactions.

Pros

You get immediate feedback about your product or service and can then adjust it in the light of comments and other feedback.

Cons

You might not have enough time to evaluate things properly or make changes before the product or service gets sold.

Secondary sources

Secondary sources are those which have been produced by other people. They might include directories, customer lists, information from market research companies, newspapers, etc. You might need to employ a market researcher to answer some of these questions. For example, in a particular area are there many people who own dogs? Or, conversely, where do most dog owners live? Some questions can be answered by searching the internet or using a good encyclopaedia, but for others you might need to take a more sideways look.

Pros

Somebody has already done the work for you and all you have to do is find it. You can use easily available or scarcer sources depending on your needs.

Cons

It might be hard to work out what sources you need and where to find them. Costs might be high if you need to consult works by academic, business or market research organizations. The information might not be in a useable form and you might therefore need to translate it into graphs, prose or maps to interpret it.

> **BUSINESS PLAN TIP**
> Do as much desk (secondary) research as possible, including internet research, before using primary (field) research methods. You might find most of your questions answered and more quickly.

Customer satisfaction

Customer satisfaction should be at the heart of your business, and your plan will need to address this. This encompasses not only ensuring that what you sell is what they want but providing it in a way that they prefer and dealing with customer complaints. You need to be able to explain in your plan how you will deal with this. So, as well as the market research you have already done, you need to be able to explain:

- how you will get your product or service to your customers
- what standards you will expect from staff
- the kind of service you will provide
- how complaints will be dealt with
- your replacement/refund policy (over and above a customer's statutory rights)

Your plan should contain an explanation of how you know your product or service is what your customers want (based on your research) and how you will deal with any complaints.

Remember that your business will survive and thrive by being of service to your customers. If you do not know who they are or understand their needs and deliver what they want or expect, your business will not flourish.

Customer viewpoint

Look at what you sell from your customers' viewpoint. Are you simply providing what you *think* they want or have you analysed your research and found out what they *really* want and what they consider the important features are. You might discover, for example, that while you think they will be impressed by the colour or by the price, that they really value the after-sales service and size.

Ten things that customers want

Here are some common things that customers look for:

1 quality
2 value for money
3 availability
4 excellent service
5 fast supply
6 excellent after-sales care
7 fast and courteous complaints system
8 information
9 contact by phone with real people
10 guarantees

Calculating total demand

You will need to justify your choice of customers, that is the segments of the market you are aiming at, by showing what the demand for your product or service will be. Your plan should include an indication of the total demand for your product or value of the market. This is done using a particular market segment (or for some businesses, your total market) over a specific period of time (often one year) in specified market conditions. To calculate this you need to multiply the number of target customers by the number of products or number of times your service is used over the course of a year by the average price per item or service. So if you estimate there are 20,000 potential customers in a particular geographical area you are targeting and they each buy six products or services each year at £45 a time then the total market value is:

Potential customers × (number of product/service per year per customer × price of product service)

For example:

$$20,000 \times (6 \times £45) = 20,000 \times £270 = £540,000$$

You can also calculate the value as a percentage of customer spending in that sector of the market.

Test

(See page 198 for answers.)

1 What is market research?
2 Name five facts you need to know about your customers.
3 What is segmentation?
4 Name three methods of researching your customers.
5 What should your business priority be?
6 Name a useful comparison of business status.
7 How do you calculate total demand?

Plan preparation

Write a paragraph describing who your customers will be and how they are segmented. Explain why your product or service will attract them and how you will reach them and deal with them. Include the value of the market. Use the 'Ten things that customers want' checklist to describe how you will ensure that your business will provide these.

Summary

Unless you know who your customers are you cannot direct your sales effort efficiently. Use market research to discover your customers' likes and dislikes and how, when and where they want to obtain your product or service. Decide how you will deal with any complaints. Your plan needs to show that there is a market for what you sell and that the demand will be long-term.

05
marketing strategy

In this chapter you will learn:

- how to understand the market
- how to analyse the competition
- how to choose a pricing policy
- how to promote your business
- how to determine personnel and costs

You need to convince lenders or investors that you understand the market in which your business will compete. You will also need to explain how you will let people know about your product or service and convince them to buy it. In this chapter we will look at what a marketing strategy is and its various elements. We will discuss what you need to say about it in your business plan.

What is marketing strategy?

Many people think that marketing consists only of the promotional and publicity activity which is the public side of any effort to attract and keep customers. In reality, it is much more than that. It is part of an overall strategy to put the needs of the customer first. Your marketing starts with a marketing plan which will set out what you hope to achieve by marketing – who you hope to market to, what share of the market you hope to obtain, how you will promote your product or service and the timescale for achieving this. You need to explain why you are choosing to target a particular section of the market first.

Successful marketing therefore involves finding out:

- what customers think of a product or service
- who buys it
- the effects of the competition
- how to promote what you sell

You need to match the product or service to the market segments you identified in the previous chapter. Marketing also includes successfully involving staff, an efficient process and suitable physical environments whether for retail or production.

Marketing objectives

Your objectives when creating a marketing strategy need to cover all of the marketing areas. They will include objectives for the short, medium and long term. Your objectives should include:

- finding out what customers need
- assessing the competition
- deciding which areas of the market to exploit
- testing the product or service with prospective customers

Marketing factors

The success of your marketing strategy will depend on some or all of these factors:

- an enticing image
- price and service standards
- adequate and successful testing
- encouraging repeat purchases
- effective distribution
- motivated salespeople
- motivated staff
- apt packaging
- suitable environment
- efficient processes
- available credit
- ability to adapt to customers' needs

Other factors might be relevant depending on the type of business. Make sure you find out what they are.

Understanding the market

You first need to understand what the market situation is now and what trends and influences will affect your business. The research you have done to find out who your customers are and what they want (see Chapter 4) will be an important part of your marketing plan. You also need to find who your competitors are and what you can offer that they do not. Before you can explain your marketing strategy you need to show that you understand your market and will be pitching sales and promotional strategy correctly. You will need to demonstrate to your potential backers that you will be using appropriate forms of marketing to reach your customers. You also need to show that you have researched what price your product or service will comfortably sell at in today's market. These are the things that a business plan should include:

- awareness of market conditions
- who your market is and proof that it exists, i.e. are you selling to individuals or organizations and which ones?
- who your competitors are and how you will be/are different
- an estimate of your expected market share (i.e. how much of the market will you get)
- proof that your pricing policy is correctly pitched

- how you will promote the product or service (including evidence of its USP)
- how and where you will sell and distribute the product
- who will deal with the marketing
- details of longer term plans for the business
- costs associated with your marketing strategy
- details of orders that you have already received, if any

What is happening in your market?

You need to show that you have a wide understanding of the market in which your business will be competing. What are the major trends that will affect your business? What outside influences will there be? What kinds of businesses will you be competing with and where will yours fit in? Consider the structure of competition. Look at the size and type of the competition. Is there a monopoly? Or several major business groups? Or is there one dominant supplier amongst medium-size businesses? Or are there lots of small businesses? Where will your business fit into this?

Trends

It is very important to have an awareness of the major trends that affect your market. These might be as self-evident as the major festival seasons, or relationship to college terms or the football season, or more irregular trends such as a new interest in technology, environmental concerns, or a change in house prices. Trends can affect several areas of your marketing strategy:

- type of customers
- market size
- prices
- competition
- technology

You can get information about market trends from the internet, business and trade magazines, government publications and so on. If the trend is relevant to your business you will need to include a chart showing the trend in your business plan.

BUSINESS PLAN TIP
Look for relevant charts of trends in trade and business magazines and include them in your plan with references.

Market conditions

The plan will need to show that you are aware of other restraints or forces affecting your business. For example, the political climate might not be right, there might be a downward or upward turn in the economy forecast, new laws might have been introduced for your type of business, there might be geographical limitations, and so on. You might not be able to comment on these in detail, but your plan should at least show that you are aware of them and how you will deal with them. You can get information from government departments, the internet and trade and business magazines.

Outside influences

You also need to understand what outside influences there will be on your business. These might be:

- social
- political
- economic
- government

Social

The social influences that might affect your business are such things as customer expectations, new moral stances (more enthusiasm for non-smoking or anti-fur activism, for example), ethical trading considerations or environmental concerns.

Political

The political situation can affect your business both directly and indirectly. Changes in government will mean changes in attitudes to business as will legislation from the European Union. On the other hand, government attitudes to issues and the electorate's reaction can affect your business (for example, reactions to GM food). If you sell internationally the changing political situation in other countries can alter the way you do business there, or even whether you do business there at all.

Economic

The economic influences on the market are such things as the exchange rate and who has the spending power. For example, children have 'pester power' and the 'grey pound' is an acknowledgement that many older people now have considerable disposable income.

Government

The government can change such things as business rates, planning laws, licensing requirements for your type of business, standards for products and services, health and safety rules and grant regulations. It can also provide help for certain types of businesses, in the form of grants or loans (see useful organizations listed in Taking it Further). There is a huge amount of information about these influences produced by government agencies, researchers, businesses and so on. It can be overwhelming, but you need to find out what is required for your business in the market you intend to sell to.

New technology

New technology in the form of increased internet competition and more competitive processes means that you need to keep up-to-date in this area. Any business needs an internet presence to compete effectively. You need to be aware of the technology that is used in your industry and explain how you will keep up with it.

The four Ps of marketing

Your plan should include information based on the four Ps of marketing, that is *product*, *price*, *promotion* and *place* (distribution).

- product – what you are selling
- price – how much is the selling price
- promotion – how you get customers to buy
- place – where and how you will sell

Product

Examine your product's or service's features, benefits, quality, style, range, packaging, guarantees, availability and after-sales service – in fact anything that makes what you are selling attractive to customers.

Price

Here you need to be clear about how you will set your prices, what your credit deals are, what profit margins you want and how you will offer value for money. You need also to explain why and how your prices are set in relation to those of your competitors.

Promotion

You need to be clear about how you will promote your product or service, how far geographically your promotion will extend, and what budget you will allocate for this.

Place

This includes not only where you will sell but where your customers are and what distribution methods you will use.

Your target markets

You have already discovered who your customers are and that the market for your product or service exists. Provide a breakdown of your customers – for example, by age, geographical distribution or approximate income. If you have not already done so, use the information about your customers and the research into your competitors to predict what share of market you expect to achieve. For example, you might expect to achieve an almost 100 per cent share of any picture framing business in a town where none already exist, but only a very small share of one in a large city where there are many and transport links are good.

Analysing the competition

We have already looked at the importance of knowing your competition in Chapter 3. In this chapter we ask you to find out in more detail who your competitors are and how your product or service will compare with them. If you fail to include an analysis of the competition in your business plan, potential backers will not take it seriously. You need to explain how your business has or will obtain a competitive advantage in the market.

Is there really no competition?

Many people new to business make the mistake of underestimating the competition or simply declare that there is none. There is always either existing or potential competition from somewhere. Even if there seems to be no obvious competition at the moment, be sure that in the future there will be. You need to explain in your plan who your competition is and how your business will have the advantage.

Who are the competition?

You cannot simply find out the names of your competitors and think that your work is done. You need to understand clearly what they are offering so that you can ensure that you can do better or different. Your first job should be to find out the number of competitors you have, but that alone will not tell you what you have to compete with. You need to ask the following questions about their businesses:

• what exactly are their products or services?
• are they the same or different from yours?
• do they provide something that you don't?
• who are their customers?
• will you be competing for the same customers?
• what market share do they have?
• can you get some of their market share?
• how do they handle promotion and distribution?
• what standards of service and customer care do they offer?
• what new ideas are they developing?
• what special features do their products or services have?
• what are your competitors' market positions?

It is this level of analysis that will enable you to position your business idea to the best possible effect.

Stopping competitors poaching

It is important to explain in your business plan how you will stop your competitors poaching your customers. Any potential investors or lenders will need to be reassured that you have a strategy in place for keeping your share of the market and indeed growing within it. You also need to explain the *barriers to entry*. These are areas where your competitors might have the advantage and you will have to explain in your plan how you will deal with them.

Barriers to entry

Your business plan must show that you understand what barriers to entry there are. In other words, what are the main difficulties you will face in trying to enter the market. In your plan you will need to explain what they are and how you will overcome them. These might not be insurmountable problems, but they nevertheless might make entry into the market difficult unless addressed early.

These are some of the main barriers to entry:

1 setting-up costs, e.g. high costs of plant and equipment
2 technology – not being up-to-date, or not having enough equipment
3 economies of scale
4 ongoing costs
5 making your product or service different – the USP
6 distribution/buying disadvantages
7 legalities, e.g. licensing restrictions
8 market reactions and share
9 brand recognition – problems building and maintaining it
10 location – best areas possibly too expensive
11 access to scarce resource

Setting-up costs

If you cannot financially handle the setting-up costs your competitors will poach your customers while you try to get established. Make sure that you can justify the costs and that you can set up your business within a reasonable timescale.

Economies of scale

Existing businesses similar to yours which need a high volume will already have the workforce and larger facilities necessary to obtain this. If your business will require a high volume to be successful, you will need to explain in your plan how you will achieve this.

Ongoing costs

Existing businesses might already have negotiated better financial deals with suppliers and distributors. You need to understand how your business will compete with this.

Making your product or service different

The USP for your business idea might sustain its customer appeal to start with, but eventually other companies will start to produce something similar. How will you keep your customers from using another company? How will you keep your product or service different from the rest?

Distribution

For some methods of distribution you will be competing with established businesses. To obtain the same level of service you might have to pay more than you would like. Can you afford to do this? Have you other means of distribution available? If you can't get your product or service to the customers they will go elsewhere.

Legalities

Don't wait until you have started your business to find out whether there are government restrictions on any part of it. Check with your local authority, government departments and any other relevant organizations about what regulations you need to comply with. Your competitors will already have dealt with these and found ways of complying that keep their businesses competitive. Make sure you do the same. Explain in your plan what these restrictions are and how you will deal with them.

Market reactions

The entry of your business into the market is hardly going to be warmly welcomed by the competition. They might try all kinds of means to ease you out such as price wars or cutting exclusive deals with suppliers and distributors.

Researching your competitors

Researching your competitors is done in a similar way to the market research methods about customers (as shown in Chapter 4). Knowledge of your competitors is vital to see how their business offerings and methods compare with yours. You also need to do some basic research to discover where people normally buy your product and service and who from. You also need to find out what they like and dislike about any rival's offerings and what they would ideally like to see from yours. Some methods for finding out about your competitors are:

- talking to competitors' customers
- rivals' literature and websites
- market researcher
- trying competitors' product or service yourself

Talking to competitors' customers

A good way of finding out what customers think of your competitors is simply to ask them. Go to places where your competitors' product or service is being offered and talk to people who have used it or are about to use it. Ask them why they choose that company, what they like about the product or service, what do they think of your competitors' prices, quality, customer service standards and after-sales care. You will then have a good idea of what to change in your business to make it competitive.

Rivals' literature and websites

There is nothing stopping you obtaining any literature that your competitors produce so that you can gauge their strengths and weaknesses. This might include brochures, advertising and company reports. You can also look in the trade or business magazines to see whether there are any articles about the companies.

BUSINESS PLAN TIP
Send off for information offered by competitors. You will not only get written details but an idea of how efficient their marketing and customer services are. Try out their information phone lines too.

It is also possible to discover a great deal about businesses, large and small, from the internet. Most major companies will have websites, as will many smaller ones. Don't just read the main public pages but look at the press pages and company information sections. Particularly useful are the mission statements which state the USPs of the businesses. You can judge from these how your business will be different or better – or, of course, both.

Market researcher

If you want a professional report on your competitors then you need to employ a market researcher or market research company. You can find these through the market research organizations (see Taking it Further). This might be an expensive option for a small one-person business but very useful and cost-effective for a larger business aiming at investment from venture capitalists.

Try it yourself
There is nothing stopping you trying out your competitors' product or service yourself. It is the quickest way to find out exactly what they offer and how it compares with what your business will offer. Being one of their customers or potential customers means that you can legitimately ask lots of penetrating questions.

Your market share

You need to show that you understand realistically how much of the market share your product or service will expect to gain initially and over a period of time. You can gauge this by reading company reports and looking at the company websites on the internet. In a saturated market (yet another television set or yoga class) your share will be much smaller than if you have few potential competitors (a yellow weevil-shaped garden rake or a daily make-up service). On the other hand, there might still be a demand for your business idea even in a crowded market if the market is still growing.

Pricing policy

The amount of market share you have estimated as well as your potential customers will dictate the price you will charge. You need to balance the price with quality. Will you be cutting quality to sell the product or service cheaper and undercut competitors, or will you be pricing it for a more discerning market and relying on quality to attract customers? Will you be pricing it at a similar level to your competitors and offering something unique? If you will be undercutting your competitors you will have to show how you will make a profit, and if you will be charging more you will need to demonstrate the unique selling point (USP) that will encourage customers to favour you over your competitors. One way of testing prices is to hold a few test sales in temporary retail outlets to discover whether you are pitching the price correctly. You also need to show that if your pricing policy proves inaccurate that you have provided forecasts at different prices. Remember that you cannot always simply sell at the production cost plus an add-on sum for profit. If your competitors are selling at lower than that you will have to cut your prices to stay in the market, unless you are selling something so unique that you can set your own prices.

Pricing system

In your plan you need to include a section explaining your pricing system and how it relates to the prices your competitors charge. You need to justify the price and explain what you would do if competitors changed their prices.

It is better not to cut prices too low to begin with because that will leave you less room to manoeuvre if your competitors reduce their prices. It can also be hard to raise prices later when customers have come to expect low prices from you. However, you need to ensure that your prices are set so that they compare favourably with the competition. If they are set lower than just covering costs, you need to work out whether you can sustain this level of pricing financially.

Your prices will be affected by your marketing and vice versa. As you have to include information about your marketing policy in your plan, you need to explain how your prices will be affected by the level of promotion. It will also be affected by what customers expect to pay for similar products or services. You might use other promotional activities rather than low prices at start-up to avoid setting your prices too low initially.

Product life

You will need to explain how your product or service will go on being saleable after the launch. Therefore you need to work out the product's life. Ask these questions:

1 how original or unique is it?
2 will it be used only once or more than once?
3 how will competitors react to it?
4 can it be altered to prolong its life?
5 will the customer base remain the same?

Bear in mind that there are generally five stages to the life of anything sold:

1 research and development (R&D)
2 launch
3 growth
4 saturation
5 demise

Promotional activities

Once you have decided what your product or service will be, you need to find ways of getting it noticed by the general public and keeping it in the public's mind. Unless people know what you are offering they cannot buy it. Once your product or service is being sold you need to keep it in front of the public's eye so that they return to it again and again. You also need to have a clear timescale in mind for each marketing activity. Will you start with one method for a few weeks and then change to another? Will you run several marketing activities in tandem? How long will you engage in each type of activity?

Look at the various types of marketing media and decide which would be most suited to your business. A large business might use advertising in the press and on television and the radio as well as PR events. A small business might use press releases, phone-in radio programmes, and leaflets in the high street to get its message across.

There are a number of ways of promoting a product or service and these are discussed below. Not all of them will be suitable or affordable for your business, but you should explain in your business plan which you will be using for promotional purposes and why they will be effective. To launch your business idea you need to:

1 define the USP
2 create an image for your product or service
3 ensure excellent customer service
4 arrange promotion
5 arrange publicity
6 have an excellent after care policy

Getting information to your customers

You need to understand how customers will get information about your business. You will need to take these methods into account in your marketing strategy and cost them in your business plan.

- advertising (paid promotion)
- publicity
- personal contacts (word of mouth)
- salesperson
- other promotional ideas

Brand image

To sell effectively you need to create a brand or image that customers will associate with what you sell. This can be used in promotional activities. Sometimes it is put into more tangible form. Examples are a company logo or a recognizable advertising theme. Sit down and think what kind of brand image your business as a whole and each product or service in particular should have, and then brainstorm ways that you might convey that image or brand awareness to customers.

AIDA

You need to organize promotion and publicity so that customers are keen to buy what you offer. Your plan will need to include details of your promotion and publicity strategy. One way to do this is to focus on AIDA, that is *Attention, Interest, Desire, Action*. Explain in your plan:

- how you will attract customers' *attention*
- how you will stimulate and maintain their *interest*
- how you will make them *desire* what you offer
- how you will encourage them to translate that desire into the *action* of buying what you offer

Promotion consists of many elements but the main ones are advertising and publicity.

Advertising

Many people confuse advertising and publicity. But although they seem similar they are different. Advertising is paid for by the client whereas publicity is free. Advertising can be done in any part of the media but not all will be appropriate for you. If you are a small business or just starting out using the small ads, trying to get good publicity may be more effective and cheaper than paying for advertising. The following take advertisements:

- newspapers – local, trade, national, international, magazines (the costs of advertising in the press varies with the status of the production – a full-page ad in a Sunday supplement will cost more than one in a small local newspaper; small ads are very cheap but most papers ask traders to admit to the fact and mark the ad accordingly)
- radio – local, national (this is cheaper than advertising on television but you may need to pay for an actor to read it)
- television – only very large companies can afford television advertising because of the huge costs
- other means, e.g. van signs, business cards, leaflets, hoardings

If you are a franchisee then the franchisor will provide advertising and promotional material that is acceptable to the franchise as a whole. If you want to use your own promotional material or arrange advertising yourself you will need to get it approved by the franchisor. This is so that the franchise maintains its overall image.

Be honest

You must be able to justify any claims that you make in advertising under the Trades Description Act and Advertising Standards Authority Code of Practice. You can get advice about this from your local Trading Standards Office (see Taking it Further for website with details of local offices).

Publicity

Publicity is achieved through unpaid mention or recommendation by others. Because no money changes hands it is perceived by the public (sometimes erroneously) to be unbiased and therefore a more reliable judgement on a business. There are several ways of gaining publicity for a business. Most of them involve some basic costs such as postage or phone calls and these must be included in your marketing budget.

Press releases

The basis of free publicity is the press release. This provides news about your product or business or its personnel to the media, and if a journalist considers it interesting enough a story will be created from it. You may even get a photograph in the press. Publicity is generally considered better than advertising because it is deemed more objective and therefore more trustworthy.

Articles

Articles are another way of getting your business noticed by the media. If you can write a straightforward piece about a new aspect of your business you may be able to place it in the press. Call up editors and offer a piece but don't expect to get paid. Keep to any guidelines about length and deadlines. Where possible include add-ons such as a brief biography or boxes of further information. Don't forget small presses, for example newsletters, club magazines, university/school magazines, etc.

Publicity events

These can be anything that might engender publicity in the media, such as demonstrations, exhibitions, events for journalists and sponsored sports. For example, taking your product or service to halls, rooms, meetings, etc., and demonstrating it to the public can be a very effective way of promoting your product or service. Take samples of your product and hand out leaflets. At exhibitions ensure that all relevant information is available. Exhibitions can be expensive but useful for getting known.

Leaflets/catalogues

Simple leaflets can be created either on your computer or by professionals and these can be used for direct mailing or handed out for example at lectures or demonstrations. If you have more than one product or different aspects of your service to sell, you may need a catalogue. This can be a simple photocopied booklet or a full-colour production.

Direct Mailing

Direct mailing is a recognized and well-used way of looking for customers. You can buy a mailing list from agencies or create your own. There are mailing list agencies that will send your promotional material to your list for you. You and the agency must comply with the Data Protection Act. Direct mail needs to be targeted; it is a waste of time sending a mailing to everyone. Compile a list of prospects from trade directories, trade journals, yearbooks, and include previous clients, lists from mailing brokers.

Internet

You can use the internet for marketing in two ways. First, you can create your own web-page (or get someone to design one for you). Remember to put in your contact details and if necessary arrange online buying. Offset costs by links to other sites. Second, you can use e-mail to contact your customers. This is cheap and quick but remember Spam (unsolicited mail), is illegal. If you use e-mail, take care with the subject line and keep it brief. Include a link to your website, if you have one.

Special offers, free gifts

By encouraging your customers to try your product or service by using special promotions you hope to entice them to become regular customers. You might want to hand out free gifts – for example, pens, mugs, mouse mats – or sell two for one for a week.

Word of mouth

This is one of the most effective of marketing tools, and includes:

- networking – talk about your product to everyone
- business cards – these should include contact details and be landscape and standard sized; they can include a picture; remember to carry it with you at all times
- postcards – these should use a picture on one side and include all your contact details; you could also include a questionnaire
- lectures – when giving a lecture, always take a leaflet and your product with you
- badges – these might be old-fashioned, but kids like them
- balloons – always popular and eye-catching

References

If possible, get written testimonials or endorsements from individuals and companies who either use or would like to use your product or service. With their permission you can use them in your marketing activities. Any such written praise should be included in your business plan in an appendix. This will show your potential backers that your ideas go beyond just your immediate circle and will or do appeal to a wider audience.

Salespeople

If you use salespeople they can promote your business wherever they go. They can do so in retail outlets, door-to-door or as sales reps, whichever is relevant. They can answer questions and provide you with immediate feedback.

Other ideas

There are many other ways of attracting attention to your business. Some of these are:

- sponsorship
- listings in yearbooks, business directories, e.g. Yellow Pages
- promotional gifts
- public speaking
- letters to the press
- volunteering

Businesses will often use a number of methods. Decide which will suit your business best and cost it. Many will be cheap – for example, letters to the press, e-mail questionnaires. Others will be expensive – for example, magazine advertising.

Tip

If you intend to do your own promotion, concentrate on areas with which you feel most comfortable, for example, writing press releases if you hate public speaking. You will do better in publicity areas where you feel most relaxed. You can always arrange for somebody else to do the kind of publicity you hate.

Place – where will you sell it?

The detail of where you will operate will be discussed in Chapter 7, but for the purposes of your marketing strategy you will need to explain where you will sell your product or service. Explain whether you will be operating from home or elsewhere, and where you expect to sell – locally, nationally, worldwide? How will you get your product to your customers – retail premises, post, van delivery?

Locally, nationally, worldwide?

Be clear about whether you are aiming to sell your product or service locally or further afield, perhaps nationwide or even internationally. That is, do you expect your customers to live close to your business premises, or are you prepared to sell to customers much further away? How will you sell to distant customers? How will you get your product or service to them?

Sales premises

Consider the following points when deciding on where to sell your product or service from:

- shop – how will you get your shop noticed by potential customers – press, advertising, special days?
- from home – will you expect customers to come to you? Have you got a separate room or building? Will you post things out?
- take to client's home – will you take a service into a client's home, e.g. a personal hairdressing service?
- door-to-door – will you sell door-to-door or employ people to do so for you?
- telephone sales – can you use your own staff or will you employ a call centre? You will need to buy lists and understand the Data Protection Act
- direct from factory – do you have a specific workplace outside the home where the product is created? If so, will customers be allowed to visit it?
- temporary retail premises – e.g. car boot sales – suitable for small businesses; can you use short-let shop premises or a market stall?
- car boot and other sales – for small-scale business start-up, these can be good as a way of testing price and market

Monitoring and reviewing

The best marketing plans include processes for monitoring and reviewing the progress of any marketing activity. Any marketing should be monitored regularly so that any faults in the process can be quickly corrected and the activity kept on schedule. There should be regular reviews of progress so that the programme can be adapted to changing conditions and reactions from the public. The results of these processes should be recorded regularly so that they can be shown to everyone involved and the results can form the basis of an improved strategy.

Dealing with public response

It is common mistake, particularly in smaller businesses, to be overwhelmed by an unexpectedly high response to a marketing campaign. Before you start you will need to have strategies in place for responding to any unexpected demand or complaints from the public. This should be included in your business plan. For example, if the demand is good can you provide the product or service quickly enough? Can your distribution handle an increased order book? Have you got people to answer phone calls, letters and e-mails quickly? Is there a complaints procedure in place? Your business reputation will suffer if your marketing campaign is a success but you can't fulfil promises.

Marketing personnel

You should be clear about what personnel you need to implement your marketing strategy. Will you do it all yourself, enlist your family and friends, employ a marketing manager and staff? Much will depend on the size of your business and your financial expectations. However, do not make the mistake of assuming that marketing is an unimportant part of a business. Large companies will not make that mistake but smaller ones often think that a one-off campaign will suffice. Marketing must be an ongoing activity and it will cost money. First, unless marketing is ongoing, customers will soon forget your existence. Second, the market changes and your marketing strategy will need to adapt to new circumstances. Entrepreneurs are often surprised at the amount of time and energy, not to mention money, has to go into ensuring that a business has a presence in the market. In your plan include not only short-term aims – the start-up and first few months of marketing – but also longer-term plans for when your business is established. Unless you truly think that you will be able to deal with it adequately yourself, you will need to employ someone else to deal with it. That has to be factored into your business plan.

Costs of a marketing strategy

Even the most cost-effective of promotion and publicity campaigns will cost money. This will not only include the actual tools you use but also things such as time, travel, printing and employing others for the campaign. You will need to provide a realistic breakdown of marketing costs both for the initial launch and for ongoing use. Here are some typical types of marketing costs. When you add them up be realistic. For example, you may get publicity for free, but you will incur a minimum outlay for printing, postage/internet charges and phone calls. You should also include the estimated cost of your time or the actual cost of paying someone else to do the work. Even if you choose to do the work yourself it is still costing the business money in terms of work you are not doing elsewhere. You should factor into the estimated cost of promotion items such as:

- press, radio and television advertising
- postage (for direct mail, press releases, etc.)
- printing
- phone bills
- mailing list fees
- Data Protection Act fee
- transport
- internet fees – if using web or e-mail
- retail outlets
- rent of hall for demonstrations
- production base rent

Doing it right

Whatever promotional activities you decide to pursue you need to ensure that you do not fall foul of the law or mislead the public. There are certain things you must do. First you must comply with the Data Protection Act. If you keep a mailing list for direct mail advertising, for example, you may well have to pay a fee to the Data Protection Agency as well as comply with rules about removing people from the list and gaining permission for their inclusion. If individuals, for example, have given you permission to use their testimonials as long as they are kept anonymous, then you must ensure that their names do not appear on any publicity or advertising. There are also laws governing advertising, both its contents and its use. For instance, there are rules about from whom and how money may be received from advertisements in payment of a product or service. Failure to comply with the law or basic moral codes can lead to litigation. It is cheaper and safer to comply than to pay hefty fees to a court of law.

The rules for promotion and publicity are simple but sensible:

- tell the truth
- don't exaggerate
- don't mislead the public
- be clear

Test
(See page 198 for answers)
1 What four areas of business do marketing trends affect?
2 Name four areas of influence on businesses.
3 What are the four Ps of marketing?
4 Name five barriers to entry into a market.
5 What are the two types of market research?
6 How many stages are there to a product's life?
7 What does AIDA stand for?

Plan preparation

Write a description of the current state of the market you hope
to enter and what trends and influences are likely to affect it. Use
graphs and diagrams where applicable and any statistics you
have researched (remember to put in the references). Explain
your pricing policy and promotion campaign. Describe the competition and explain how you will stop them poaching your customers. Note what your sales are likely to be and how you would
deal with an overwhelming response.

Try to explain things as clearly as possible but provide enough
detail so that readers can understand what you intend to do. A
few paragraphs should be enough.

Summary

You need to understand your market before you can market your
product or service. This involves finding out about trends and
influences that affect the business and analysing the competition.
Once you have done this you can decide which marketing
methods to use. Your business plan will contain a description of
the market and the competition and your marketing strategy,
including promotion.

06

managing your business

In this chapter you will learn:

- how to discover your leadership skills
- how to decide what personnel you need
- how to decide what skills your business needs
- how to treat and motivate your staff
- the legal basics you need to consider
- how to determine service standards

Once you have got a businesses plan, who will put its contents into action? In your business plan you will need to convince the readers that your business will be managed by the most appropriate people and in the most effective manner. You need to explain who will manage the business and what they will do, how the business will be administered, how employees will be involved in the business, what training staff will need and who your suppliers will be. In other words, this part of the business plan will discuss the people involved in running your business.

The way your business is managed will affect its efficiency, the type and number of staff, staff costs and the type of product or service you can offer.

First and foremost any investor will want to know whether your business has the skills to deliver the plan. Those skills will be provided by you and any partners or employees, so you must ensure that you can convince investors that the necessary skills will be available. You need to work out:

1 what skills your business needs
2 who will deliver them
3 whether training will need to be provided

Don't forget yourself

Little Noddy, when asked to count how many people there were on a picnic, kept getting the wrong answer because he forgot to include himself. Remember that if you are part of the management team, you need to include your own details in the business plan. If you are watching the business from the sidelines you will still need to inform readers who you are and why you are presenting the plan. If you are in charge of the business then you will need to have an overview of the business and readers will expect to see that reflected in the plan. Other attributes you should have include:

• profession/trade understanding
• an understanding of the market and how your business works
• promotional strategy
• ability to manage the money (overall, even if you leave the details to others)
• people skills

If you have not got these overall skills you must explain in the plan how you intend to obtain them for your business and which of your managers and staff will use these skills.

You as leader

In the plan you should not only describe your skills and expertise but explain how you will be leading the company, if that will be your role. The success of a business depends very much on the personality of the person at the top and how that is communicated through management to staff. How do you see yourself acting in the role of leader or a partner? You will need to show that you have an understanding of the business as a whole and that you have an excellent understanding of the business. You need to know the limitations of the business too. Investors will not be impressed by a plan which shows that you will be over-reaching the boundaries of a business of your type. You need to have an overall understanding of how to market your business and manage the money, even if you won't be dealing with those aspects personally. Above all you need to show that you can manage people if you will have employees or partners. Even the most dictatorial of business owners need to be able to communicate effectively with other people.

Checklist

Do you think you have the qualities necessary to take on the leadership role in a business? Which of these best describes your personality? Tick all that apply.

☐ dictatorial
☐ prefer to work alone
☐ consensual
☐ team-worker
☐ calm
☐ confrontational
☐ risk-taker
☐ hands-on
☐ attentive to detail
☐ take a broad view
☐ confident
☐ need support
☐ knowledgeable about the business

There are no right or wrong answers to this. But by pinpointing honestly your personality traits you can see whether you have all the necessary leadership skills. If you do, you can approach your business confidently; if not, you need to employ managers who have the personality traits that you do not and delegate.

On your own

If you will be managing the business on your own it might be hard to convince people in a position to help that you alone have all skills and experience to run your business without other managers. This is particularly difficult if you do not have the relevant experience but are convinced that you can make the business a success. In your plan you will need to demonstrate to readers that you have other equivalent experience. You should include references from people who can confirm that you have skills or qualifications that are equally useful and relevant. It is worth including these, even if they do not relate exactly to the business. If you think that, even so, readers would not be impressed with your present skills, it might be wise to defer presenting your business plan until you can take some training that will improve your claim. In any case, if you do not have formal training in business or management it would be sensible to take basic short courses in these subjects before starting your business. Many colleges and evening institutes run short courses on many useful subjects – everything from basic word processing and IT skills to book-keeping or trade and professionally based courses, including NVQs, HNCs and degrees.

Working with others

If you will have partners or intend to employ managers you need to be able to stress the skills they will bring to the company. Ideally, have key managers identified so that you can stress their skills and include their CVs and references in the plan. You should explain exactly who will do what and explain how individuals will resolve any weaknesses in your management structure.

Be realistic

Although in your plan you need to be positive, be careful not to overplay your strengths. You might be able to bluff your way on paper or at a face-to-face meeting, but potential lenders or investors will make thorough background checks. If you overestimate your strengths or those of your managerial team, you will be found out. You need to take a careful look at what strengths your business needs and either recruit managers with skills to fill the gaps or arrange a group of advisors to provide the skills you or your team lack.

Your personnel

Who will be managing your business? This is a basic question that you need to answer. You might be running it on your own, in which case you will need to explain how you will manage not only providing the product or service yourself, but how you will deal with the administrative tasks (all that paperwork and all those phone calls) by yourself. Although your business plan will concentrate on the key managers for your business, you need to decide what other staff you need and how many.

If you will be running the business on your own then you will need to decide the number and skills of the managers you need. If you are running it with one or more partners you may divide certain skills amongst yourselves or employ others as well. These might include:

- secretaries/administrators
- salespeople
- marketing personnel
- production staff – in the factory/on the shop floor
- research and development
- warehouse/stock control staff
- distribution/delivery staff
- financial staff for accounting, sales orders, processing and invoicing
- supervisory staff
- personnel/recruitment manager

As well as knowing what kind of staff you need, you also need to be able to state certain basic information about them. This will include:

- number of staff in total/for each skill/section/for each period of the plan (perhaps fewer while starting)
- skills the business needs
- level of qualification/skills needed
- costs of salaries and wages
- method of recruitment
- type of employee sought

Number of staff

You might start with a certain number of employees but expect to increase the number as your business expands. At each stage you need to be able to say how many staff you need for each kind of job and why you need that number then.

Consider the costs of the number of staff you have in mind. Do you need them all? Or would it be more cost-effective to out-source to others? For example, you might be able to eliminate salespeople if you use specialist agencies, wholesalers or distrib-utors. Look at how the competition deals with staffing. Can you do something similar?

BUSINESS PLAN TIP
Remember that in a new business staffing needs might change as the business progresses. In your business plan concentrate on start-up personnel, but include estimates of future staff increases.

Skills for your business

You must be clear about the skills your business needs in its staff. These might be practical, such as IT skills, van drivers, craft skills, or specific qualifications such as accountancy, personnel management, law, etc. As well as these skills you will need people with such things as managerial skills and promotional skills. There are five main areas of your business for which you will need skills. These are:

1 operational – that is how the business will be run on a day-to-day basis
2 technical – relevant to your particular business
3 financial
4 marketing
5 human resources

Among the skills your business might need are:

- IT expertise
- administration
- sales experience
- sales forecasting
- invoicing
- pricing policy
- tax planning
- human resources (employment/personnel)
- environment

- health and safety
- contracts
- delivery systems
- purchasing
- government legislation knowledge
- time management
- production
- marketing
- legal
- financial – including accounting
- secretarial

Your key managers may have some or all of these skills as they have to take an overall view of the business. You need to ensure that all the skills you need are available in the managers you employ and your staff.

General skills

The specific skills you will need for your business will depend on the type of business and the specific jobs within it, but most of the above skills will be necessary. Not all your employees will have all the skills, but there may well be some basic skills that you expect all your employees (and yourself) to have. These might include such skills as:

- team-working
- time management
- literacy and numeracy
- customer service

It is important to show in your plan that you know what skills your business will need in the future. So, apart from demonstrating that the business can start with the necessary skills, you must work out what additional skills the business might need later. You must then explain how you will get staff with those skills – will you recruit them? Train existing staff? Employ outside experts for the short term when necessary? All this you must decide and cost for your plan.

External help

Don't forget that you might need to involve outside help from time to time and this must be explained and accounted for and costed in the business plan. For example, you might need to employ occasionally a public relations firm, market research company, solicitor, sales reps, PR expert, accountant or patent preparer.

Qualifications

Once you know what skills you need, decide what level of qualification you will need from applicants. Will you need college certificates/diplomas/degrees, several years of expertise, professional or trade qualifications, or will you create a test for applications to pass?

Staff costs

In any business plan the costs must be spelt out clearly. Once you have decided on the number and skills of your personnel you need to work out exactly how much you will be paying them. Remember that you need to take into account not only salaries and wages but such things as National Insurance, holiday pay, sickness pay, etc.

Recruitment

How will you recruit your staff? Will you put ads in the local papers, advertise in professional magazines, put out radio ads nationwide, rely on word of mouth, employ your friends? This will take time and money and however you do it, it needs to be justified in your plan.

Type of employee

What kind of employee are you looking for? Are you looking for people with training or who are willing to learn your ways? People who work well as a team or who can work well on their own? People who are creative and energetic or reliable and efficient (possibly, but not necessarily, both)? Unless you are clear about the kind of person you want working with you, you will not get a team together that works well together.

BUSINESS PLAN TIP
Imagine you are buying your own product or service. How would you expect to be treated? Do as you would be done by.

To do

1   Make a list of all the skills both practical and managerial that your business needs.
2   List how many of the skills you have (or will use).
3   Decide how many managers you need for the business and what skills each will need – will you need one manager with several skills, or several with specific skills?
4   List the skills your employees will need and how many staff you will need.
5   Write a one-line description of the type of person you want to employ.

How you treat your staff

The success of your business will depend on how you treat your staff. This is not only how you all get on together at work but how you involve them in the business. It also includes a lot of things that are laid down by law. In your business plan you need to show that you have thought about the structure and practical side of employing staff. Once you have explained how many staff you need, with what skills, and how much they will cost, you need to explain how they will work together and how you will keep them. You might be running a business where staff stay only a short time (for example, fast food, restaurants) or one where staff stay for several years or more (for example, the professions). This needs to be taken into consideration when explaining how your business will be managed.

Just employing staff is not the end of management but the beginning. You need to consider:

• training – very important
• motivation – how to persuade staff to give their best
• keeping sickness and accident absences to the minimum
• how to deal with grievances
• how wages will be negotiated or salaries decided (e.g. will there be a bonus system, shares scheme, commission?)

Motivating managers

Managers need to be motivated so that they can motivate their staff in turn. Be supportive both of your managers and your staff. The success of your business lies largely on their shoulders. How will you motivate your managers and what will it cost? Will you offer:

- promotions
- benefits
- longer holidays
- pay rises
- shares
- company cars

BUSINESS PLAN TIP
Money is not the only motivator. Ask your managers what they
really want.

If you intend to provide any of these incentives for your managers or staff you will need to include the costs in your financial
statements.

Training

If your managers or staff do not have all the relevant skills your
business needs you will need to decide how you will deal with
training. Will you train staff on the job? Arrange day-release
courses? Provide a course of training immediately on joining the
business? Any training needs to be costed and included in your
financial statements.

Workers and the law

Even if you work by yourself there are legal aspects to be considered. At the least you need to understand what you need to do
regarding National Insurance, VAT (if relevant) and income tax.
If you employ other people then there are more aspects to be
taken into account. If you are not sure of any of these you need
to take advice from an accountant or solicitor. Depending on the
type of business you run, you will need to comply with the latest
rulings on:

- insurance
- working conditions
- maternity leave
- director's responsibilities
- keeping vital records
- statutory sick pay
- discrimination acts
- planning law/building regulations

- environmental standards
- staff and customer safety
- standards of product/service
- financial aspects
- Data Protection Act

Every part of your business might be subject to legal or financial restraints. You need to know what these are for your business and how they will affect it. It is no good claiming that you didn't comply with a law because you didn't know about it. Any one reading your plan will expect you to understand what the law requires of your business and how you are going to deal with it. To that end you might well need to employ outside advisors to ensure that you understand the law and how it relates to your business and that you are able to include how you are going to comply with the law in your plan correctly. Among issues that might need this kind of help are:

- import/export procedures
- insurance, VAT, tax
- patents, copyright, trademarks
- property – buying, leasing or renting
- discrimination, dismissal, contracts, etc.
- environmental protection
- food hygiene
- health and safety
- employment law

For example, if you are making food to sell there will be laws about food hygiene, the type of premises you use, health matters and sales law to comply with involving inspections.

For your plan you should estimate the number of staff you will employ and check with an accountant for advice about how much insurance, tax and so on will cost you per staff member. This needs to be included in your accounts.

If you will be in a business that has a trade body or professional organization then you need first to join it, and then to get advice from them about any laws that you need to comply with. For some businesses – for example, solicitors, architects – membership of the relevant professional organization is mandatory before you can start trading.

Service standards

In your plan you need not only to demonstrate how your business will be managed but also what standards you expect from your staff (including yourself and any partners). It is the people in a business who create the standards that customers see. A shoddy service or product will mean that you lose customers and the reputation of the business will suffer. The plan should demonstrate that you understand the need for standards and explain what they are and how you will attain and keep them. A successful business is one that has high standards and maintains them.

Look carefully at how you treat, or expect to treat, your customers. What standards do you expect from your staff? This might be how they look, how they speak to customers in person or on the phone, standards in responding to phone calls or letters, presentation of goods, quality of service, using initiative, and so on.

There are three important areas you need to address:

1   speed of service – will your customers get the product or service straight away, have to wait a week, or wait 28 days?
2   how to handle complaints – if you handle complaints well, customers will not only return but also praise your business to other people
3   what are your rules for payment methods – will you accept credit cards or only cheques?

In your plan you therefore need a statement about what your standards are, how you will train your staff to ensure that they meet those standards, and how you will monitor their performance.

Franchisee

If you are running a franchise, the way you manage your business will be largely determined by the franchise owner. You need to be clear about what help you can expect to get from them and whether that help will be ongoing or only during the start-up period. There might also be limitations on the amount or type of financial and other benefits that you can offer your staff. For example, their salaries, holidays and benefits may be determined by the franchise owner as part of the franchise agreement. If you are going to run a franchise you should include copies of the franchise agreement, operating rules and any other documents or manuals that the franchisor provides. As the franchisor will have had much experience of helping franchisees, you would do well to ask their help in preparing your business plan.

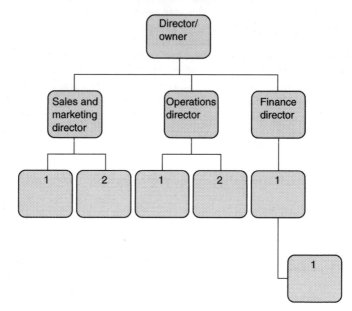

Figure 2: example management structure diagram

More work

Managing your business does not just involve knowing what your staff will be doing and dealing with the legal aspects. There are a lot of practical things that you will need to explain in your plan. For example, you need to know what you will do about the following. Have you got systems in place for:

- record keeping – customer database, sales information, government information, staff information, general
- document and letter production
- order processing
- dealing with trade unions

You will need to decide, for example, what record keeping system you will use and whether all your records will be computerised and if so which system to use and who will be in charge of keeping it up-to-date. Will you have standards for producing letters and documents and which IT packages will you use? How will you process your orders? Will your employees belong to a trade union?

Appraisal and monitoring

Readers of your plan will want to know not just who will be managing your business but how staff will be appraised and performance monitored. They will need to know that you have considered how to ensure that standards are maintained and that key staff are given opportunities for training and career advancement. The skills your business needs might change over time and you need to ensure that your managers and staff keep up with the needs of the business as far as skills are concerned.

Work out how often monitoring will be done and how it will be recorded. Remember that monitoring needs to be acted on. If standards or ways of working are not successful, you need to decide how they will be changed and what support your staff will need.

The business as a whole should be monitored against targets and objectives. This needs to be done so that you can tell whether the business is successful or whether any part of it needs changing to meet targets. In your plan you need to explain how this will be done and who will have responsibility for doing it.

Test
(See page 198 for answers.)
1 Who is often forgotten in a business plan?
2 What are the main areas of business operations?
3 What might motivate managers apart from money?
4 In what kind of business are benefits determined by someone else?
5 How can you maintain high standards among your employees?

Plan preparation

You should set out the management structure of your business (a simple diagram can help here) and state how it will be managed. You should list the skills needed and which of your staff will supply them and describe how you will deal with key issues such as training, recruitment, etc. For all staff already employed or lined up you should state which skills they will bring to the business and include the CVs of your senior management team in an appendix along with your own CV and any relevant references.

For yourself (and each key team member if relevant) provide details of their experience and skills, weakness (which will be made up by other team members) and past successes. So include:

- age
- qualifications
- experience
- description of job they will do
- brief and relevant work CV
- achievements
- expected career progression
- what strengths they will bring to the job
- their financial share in the business (if relevant)

Include information about the number of other staff you expect to employ, if relevant, and what main areas of the business they will operate in. Explain how any training will be undertaken. Include information about any necessary business legalities and how you will comply with them.

Summary

The management of your business and the number and type of staff you employ will be an important part of your business plan. You need to provide details of all your managers, including their CVs, references and qualifications. Don't forget to include details of your own expertise. The type and number of other staff you employ will depend on the type and size of your business, but this information should be included together with information about training, appraisal and monitoring of their performance. If you need to use outside experts this should be made clear. You also need to understand any legalities your business must comply with especially where it concerns your staff.

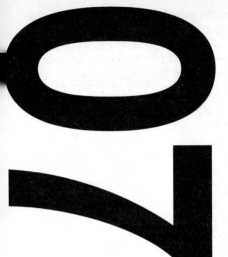

07

operating the business

In this chapter you will learn:

- the questions to ask about operating your business
- how to decide your administration needs
- how to determine when, where and how your business will operate
- how to find the most efficient operating method

You need to explain clearly how your business will operate, that is you need to explain the practicalities of how your product will be created, stored, distributed and how your staff will do this. If you are providing a service you need to explain how it will be delivered and where.

What do you know?

You probably know a great deal about your business, but might find it hard to put it into words. You need to be able to do this so that any potential investors will be reassured that you have a detailed understanding of how your business will work in day-to-day terms. There are basically five areas of operation that you need to be clear about:

- premises and location
- plant and machinery/equipment
- staff
- supply and distribution
- legalities

We have discussed management, staffing and marketing in previous chapters. Here we discuss premises, production, supply and distribution.

Questions to ask

Although you might understand how your business operates, other people won't. Think about what someone would need to know to operate your business in the same way as you do. What would you tell somebody who wanted to start in the same line of work?

Questions they might ask would be:

- What kind of premises does my business actually need? Can I work from home or do I need separate premises?
- Where will it be located? Is location important to me or my customers?
- How much space will I need for production, offices and storage?
- Is the building easily accessible (including compliance with disability access law)?
- Are there enough parking spaces and what public transport services are nearby?

- What machinery, plant or other equipment will be needed?
- Where will I get my supplies of raw materials or products from?
- How and where will I store my product or base my services?
- Will I need vehicles and if so what kind and how many?
- Will I need to hire or lease anything? If so, what will the payment terms be?
- What are the payment terms for any purchases I need to make?
- When will my operating hours be? And when will my business be available to customers? Will I need to arrange shift working for my staff?
- How will stock control be dealt with?
- How will I make my product or supply my service?
- How will I deal with supply and delivery of components to me or product or service to customers?
- Is my IT system up-to-date and adequate for my business?
- What legal requirements must I comply with?

As you try to answer these questions you might well find that you have gaps in your own knowledge. If so, write a list of questions and find out what you need to know.

Keeping up with technology

Before you look in detail at the rest of your business operation, decide from the outset how much you will use information technology (IT). Nowadays, it's a vital part of any business and you will not be competitive unless you make the best use of it. This might be as basic as using e-mail and keeping your accounts on your computer, or it might involve setting up a website and enabling online ordering or using the internet as a marketing tool. You need to consider things such as phones, fax-modems, mobile phones, networking several computers, and so on. The type of IT equipment you invest in will dictate how efficient your business is and how effective your communications are. You need to decide this at the outset so that you can include the costs in your business plan. You also need to decide whether you intend to invest in other IT equipment later and how often you will need to replace it.

You might need training to use IT equipment if you are new to it or to get the best out of existing equipment. Many people use only a fraction of their computer's power. Bear in mind that the quickest way for anyone to obtain a good understanding of how computers work is to get somebody else to show them.

In your business plan you should explain how your business will be improved by using IT and how it will make it competitive. If you can, see what IT your competitors use. For example, if they all have websites then you must have one or lose your customers to competitors with a web presence.

Administration

The administration of your business is a prime concern. All parts of your business will need to be subject to good administration practices such as invoicing, stock-taking, order processing, secretarial work, receiving stock, sales recording, accounting, warehouse processes, and so on. You need to convince readers of your plan that you know how your business will operate on a day-to-day basis. It is the administration of the business that will ensure that all parts of your business will operate efficiently. You need to decide who is going to deal with which part of the administrative process and what costs will be involved. Work out how you will organize the following:

- operations – order processing, invoicing, stock control and recording
- record keeping – accounting, reporting systems
- secretarial support – filing, photocopying, stationery, word processing
- office equipment – computer systems, photocopiers, faxes, scanners, phones, printers

You might be able to combine these jobs or equipment. But you need to work this out beforehand so that you can include the costs in your plan.

Staffing needs in general have been discussed in Chapter 6. Here you need to work out how administration needs link with other areas of the business and what training staff need. You also need to decide how to install and evaluate administration methods.

Administrative activities should make the most effective use of IT to minimize costs and time. Warehouse and production activities should be organized as efficiently as possible to reduce costs.

Premises and location

You need to consider not only where the business offices are but where any product is made or service provided. You might operate a small business entirely from your home, but if you are selling something you might need a shop. If you are providing a service you might need premises to do it from, for example running a yoga class would mean leasing a hall. A larger business might require separate office space, a factory or a large showroom.

You also need to explain how the location of your business relates to any competition. Have you leased a shop close to a similar shop to attract some of their trade, or away from them to be the first to provide it in a new area? For example, in my market town there are two supermarkets next door to each other that attract similar customers, but only one music shop with no competition for customers for miles around. Where will you locate your business – at home? A garage? A shop? A restaurant? A village hall? Or will you take your product or service to your clients?

Much will depend on the nature of your business, of course, but to save costs as your business gets under way you might be able to use space you already have for a temporary period. However, there are alternatives to the standard business premises. By thinking laterally and asking around you might find that you could, for example, rent a room from a friend, share a work space with others, rent a meeting room in a hotel, etc.

Working from home

At its most basic the location of your business could be your own home. In that case you need to explain where that is, what area of your home will be used for the businesses, how you will deal with integrating work into home life, and whether you have understood and complied with any insurance, mortgage, safety requirements that might apply. Your local authority might need to be consulted if there will be a lot of vehicles or people coming to your home; you may be subject to inspections if you intend to sell food cooked in your own kitchen.

Consider these problems:

- have you got the space to work at home and, if relevant, store products or equipment safely and securely?
- can you integrate your work and home life successfully?
- can you operate your business from your home in safety?
- is your mortgage company, landlord or council happy about the arrangements? Will you have any problems with the neighbours?

- do you need new insurance or to change existing insurance?
- can customers reach your home easily and, if relevant, is there a separate room for seeing clients?
- do you need a separate phone line?
- will your work create excessive noise or unsightly waste?
- are there any environmental aspects to be aware of?

Using other premises

For larger scale businesses or those that need separate production or retail premises you have a greater set of problems. You will need to locate premises and arrange to buy or lease them. You might need planning permission to built, extend or adapt them. You need to justify the site in relation to access to your customers and means of production. You need to ensure that your business will not disturb neighbours or cause environmental problems.

There are more technical problems to be dealt with by using a separate site. Far more regulatory controls come into play. Any or all of these might be relevant:

1 planning consent
2 listed building consent
3 building regulations
4 environmental health, including noise and pollution
5 licences for special activities
6 fire safety certificate
7 health and safety
8 insurance
9 access

Before your business starts you need to get details of these and find out how you need to comply with them. Details of any certificates you receive and consents must be included in your business plan.

Space

You might have enough space to work in at home. But there are other places where you can operate your business. If your business is small you might be able to use a garage or rent space under the railway arches. You can rent office space or perhaps use a purpose-built shed in the garden. Larger businesses might need a factory, warehouse, large offices and retail outlets.

> **BUSINESS PLAN TIP**
> Many people who run their own businesses from home find that they work better if they leave the house every day to work elsewhere. This gives a working routine to the day. Even going to work in a shed at the end of the garden creates a working atmosphere.

Place

Decide where you want the business to be located. If you are supplying goods or services that don't need you to meet customers your home might be fine. Otherwise you need to decide whether it will be located close to where your customers will be, or close to a prospective workforce, and in what relationships to your competitors.

Location costs

You need to include the costs of buildings in your business plan. This will include not only the cost of buying or leasing the premises, if relevant, but ongoing costs such as lighting or heating. You will also need to include the costs of getting the premises into a fit state for your business. You might need to pay for altering the internal layout, building additions or repairs, redecoration, soundproofing, improving access, improving lighting and heating or providing toilets. You must also consider the needs of any customers or employees who might have disabilities now or in the future and so your premises might need to be adapted for disabled access.

Plant, equipment, machinery

Even the most basic of home businesses will need some equipment – a phone and a computer as well as any machines and tools necessary for the business. Larger businesses might require heavy machinery or plant.

Your plan will need to include details of exactly what equipment or plant your business needs to operate and details of how much they will cost to buy or lease. You need to assess how much they will lose value over the years of the plan and estimate how much they will cost to replace. You will also need to supply details of the running costs of the equipment and an estimate of the costs of any peripherals that will need replacing regularly, for example, printing ink and paper for a printer, parts for machinery, etc.

If you will be using vehicles you need to take into account their cost to buy or rent, the cost of tax and insurance, petrol, replacement parts, and so on.

Storage

Many businesses do not need much storage, but even the smallest needs to store some things. Before you decide where to work, evaluate how much storage space you need. If you only need to store printer paper and toner and a few books then working from home will cause few problems for storage. If you need to store hundreds of items of raw materials for your product or boxes of the finished product, or need a lot of equipment for your service, then you will need larger storage space. This might be part of your production premises or your storage might be separate. You should work out exactly what storage space you need now and allow for increased production in the future. If you store materials or finished products away from the production process you need to take into account the cost of transporting these to and from the various sites.

Storage is subject to its own conditions. You need to pay particular attention to fire safety, insurance, and any laws governing the storage of vulnerable products such as foodstuffs or inflammable goods. Work out where your storage will be and how much it will cost to buy or lease space.

Vehicles

Using your own car to transport products or visit clients is a possibility. If you need to buy or hire other vehicles the cost of these and their running costs must be included in your plan.

Hiring and leasing

It is tempting to assume that you need to buy all your equipment, plant, buildings, vehicles, and so on, but it may well be more cost-effective to hire or lease such things. Even quite small items can be hired from specialist concerns. Sit down and work out the comparative costs of buying and leasing bearing in mind that if you buy, the value of the equipment will go down and you may have to pay more to replace it eventually, whereas if you hire or lease equipment then these can be replaced with the latest model when necessary. If you hire or lease plant, equipment, vehicles or other machinery the company hiring them out will usually repair and maintain them. Either this will be part of the fee or a there will be a separate contract for this. Some contracts will specify that repairs will be done on the premises and if the machines are irreparable they will be replaced.

Before you decide to buy anything for your business, consider first whether it would be cheaper to hire or lease. Compare prices and terms from different suppliers. Typical things that can be acquired in this way include:

- plant or heavy equipment
- computers, printers, etc.
- televisions, DVD players, video or tape recorders
- vehicles
- office furniture
- buildings
- cleaning machines

Operating hours

Part of deciding how your business will work is to decide when the business process will take place. That is, not only when the product will be produced or the service prepared but when these will be supplied to customers. For example, you might decide to run a small factory on a 24-hours-a-day timetable but only supply the product in your shops between 9 a.m. and 5.30 p.m. You might decide to do the preparation for an aromatherapy business every morning but only see clients in the afternoons five days a week. The amount of time during which you use premises for production purposes will affect the costs of such things as heating and lighting, running costs of machinery, staff wages, and so on. You must calculate these to put in your plan.

Supply and distribution

An important part of your business operation will be getting the product or service to your customers. This has two parts: first, who will supply the product or service and second, who will distribute it and how. If you intend to operate entirely on your own you still need to work out how to reach your customers. These things need to be sorted out before you submit your business plan.

Supply

Supply covers providing the product or service. If you are doing this yourself then you are the supplier. If you are buying raw materials, parts or completed products from other people, or are buying in services to sell on to your customers, then you are dealing with suppliers who can dictate the cost of these. There are several problems that need to be overcome when dealing with suppliers:

1 costs
2 payment
3 availability
4 timing
5 reliability

Costs

You need to find out whether you will be able to afford the costs of your intended suppliers, not only at start-up but as the business progresses. New businesses might have to pay more for supplies than established businesses which might have negotiated more favourable terms. You need to have located possible suppliers and ascertained what terms they will offer you so you can include them in your plan.

Payment

The payment arrangements that you make with your suppliers are very important. Whether you source from one supplier or several, the terms of payment they offer you, such as the amount of credit you are given and when you have to pay for supplies, will affect your cash flow and availability of the supplies. For example, if you have to pay for your supplies upfront and you don't get paid for your goods or services for six months this will affect your cash flow. You will need to show this in your cash flow statement (see Chapter 8).

Availability

There are several aspects to the availability of supplies. First, is the distance between you and the supplier going to cause problems with getting the supplies to you? Second, can the supplier guarantee uninterrupted supplies? Finding good supplies can be difficult but you need to get this sorted out before you submit your plan.

Timing

Even if you have located suppliers, you need to work out whether they can get the supplies to you when you need them. You should decide whether you need supplies whenever you order them, which might be at varying intervals, or will you need them at regular intervals and will store any surplus? If you decide to operate on a 'Just in Time' (JIT) system you will need suppliers who can get products to you very quickly and in orders of varying sizes according to your immediate needs.

Reliability

Once you have found suppliers who appear to fulfil your needs, you need to find out how reliable they are. Ask them how they will guarantee supplies and whether they have back-up suppliers to help out in emergencies. You need to find out:

- their contract terms
- who their main customers are
- what emergency back-up they have
- how many outlets or factories they have
- how big they are

Critical Path Analysis

To judge whether you can operate your business in the most efficient manner you can use Critical Path Analysis (CPA) to assess the whole process. You can also control projects through development from start to finish. This involves some straightforward steps and calculation:

1 break the project down into small steps
2 decide how long each step should take
3 decide the steps to be completed before others start
4 chart the project including each step

It is usual to draw a diagram to show the critical path, although it can be written as a list. The critical path is the shortest one through the process or project where each step must be completed before the next one can start. Other steps might overlap with this. The total time this path will take is how long the project will take. Using this chart you can see where steps might be shortened by more efficient working or systems. You might be able to make production more efficient by modernizing plant or processes, by using staff more effectively and efficiently. You might be able to make the process more economical by sub-contracting some parts of the project. Using Critical Path Analysis will also show you where you need to expand or modernize in the event of increased demand. Looking at the critical path will also tell you when you will need supplies or can arrange delivery. The use of JIT (Just In Time) supplies might shorten the path. The chart you create will enable you to work out the fastest and slowest completion times for the project or process and the starting and ending points for each step. By including the staff titles of those who are responsible for each stage you can monitor actions. You can see who is needed at each point. You can use this to decide what staff and management team members you actually need (see Chapter 6). CPA will enable you to set up a recording system for the whole process so that every stage can be checked and evaluated against the expected result.

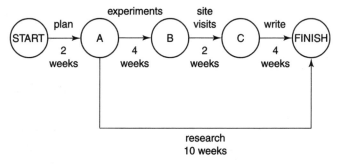

Figure 3: example Critical Path Analysis

BUSINESS PLAN TIP

Draw up a CPA for the overall business process as far as you know it at this stage. Use this to amend your business plan before presentation.

Contingency plans

Set out in your plan your contingency plans for any times that your supplier lets you down. How will you get supplies or personnel in an emergency? Have you made contact with other suppliers who could accommodate you at short notice? Have you a compensation scheme prepared for customers who are let down by your service?

Distribution

Your product or service has to get from your business to your customers and so distribution plays a very important part in your business operations. Unless you intend to handle the distribution yourself you need to rely on others to do so. The costs of this will be included in your plan. Having read the previous chapters you will have already worked out expected demand for your product or service taking into account any seasonal and other changes. You will also have decided on the geographical area of your distribution. You should now decide the level of distribution service that you will offer. For example, will you deliver on receipt of payment or within 28 days? The problems of distribution are similar to that of supply. You need to find people who are reliable to do the job and choose the most efficient method of distribution you can afford. The aspects of distribution you need to consider are:

1 method
2 costs
3 reliability

Method

You might be supplying the service or product yourself. This is perfectly possible for small personal businesses, – for example, masseur, portrait painter, self-produced CD, home-made cakes. But once your business grows or if you already plan or have a sizeable business, then methods of distribution become important. Distribution might mean getting the product directly to the customer or getting to a premises where the customer can buy it. These might include:

- retail premises, e.g. shops, cafes
- post – Royal Mail or private firm
- courier
- vehicle, e.g. van, car, lorry, motorcycle
- internet – web, e-mail
- freight – train, air, ship
- door-to-door
- house 'parties'

Many businesses will use a combination of these methods. You need to ensure that whatever distribution method you choose, it is the most effective for your business.

Costs

The method of distribution that you choose will depend to some extent on what you can afford to spend. However, you need to buy the most effective and efficient method of distribution that your business can afford and still stay in profit. A company that cannot get its product or service to the customer will not survive long. Be realistic too. The method of distribution must be suitable for what you sell. Hiring a van to transport books to individual customers when they could more easily be sent by post would be a waste of money. On the other hand, if you are supplying a bookshop, then it would be a cost-effective method. You need to work out what the minimum delivery quantities should be to be cost-effective.

Reliability

As with suppliers, you need to find a method of distribution that is reliable and, if using other people, distributors who can be relied upon.

Contingency plans

Before you submit your plan work out what you would do if your distribution method broke down. How would you reach your customers? Would you be able to deliver products yourself or send a substitute to supply a service if you work for yourself? Or can you call on other distributors at short notice? Do you have an alternative method of distribution in mind for when things go wrong?

Stock levels

Closely associated with distribution is what levels of stock you need to maintain to provide a competitive service level in the market. It is this stock level that you need to be able to maintain by your production method and for which you will need to provide adequate storage where it can be easily distributed to customers. This might be on or off any retail site.

Stock levels also relate closely to your sales. It is very important to decide how you will deal with the amount of finished products you hold. For example, will you hold just enough stock to fulfil every order, or maintain a stock level to cover all possible orders from a range? Will you create the product on demand? The more stock that you hold, the more working capital will be tied up in it.

The amount of stock that you will hold will depend on several factors. You should determine this bearing in mind:

- how much stock you want to have available for your customers
- storage space
- cost of storage
- the most economical production quantity
- shelf life of stock
- seasonal changes in demand

For many small businesses, in particular, the quality of their service might be one of their main selling points, so they need to consider very carefully the level of stock they should maintain. They need to relate this carefully to the method of distribution which can greatly affect how much stock should be held. As with larger businesses, working capital is tied up in stock so that small businesses should be aiming to reduce it as much as possible.

Research and development

Research and development is an ongoing process that is an integral part of your operations. You should be constantly striving to find new and better ways of creating, marketing and delivering your product or service. This applies as much to a small business as a large one. Any costs in terms of staff, plant, materials and so on should be included in your financial documents.

Production methods

Whether simple or complex, your production methods need to be as efficient and cost-effective as possible. Nowadays, you cannot afford out-of-date or inefficient production methods unless they are an intrinsic part of the final product or service, for example, hand-made shoes or an Indian head massage. You need to calculate when would be the earliest time to update machinery and how frequently you need to retrain staff in new methods.

Benchmarking

This is a useful way of finding out where you need to improve aspects of your business. Compare the processes and products of your business with the industry best and see whether you compare favourably. You should aim to improve on the industry average. Benchmarking gives you something to test your business against and should be an ongoing process.

Test

(See page 198 for answers.)

1 Name four areas of administration.

2 Name three regulatory building controls with which you might need to comply?

3 Give two examples of items that can be hired or leased.

4 What are the main problems you might encounter with suppliers?

5 What tool can you use to determine the most efficient operating method?

Plan preparation

Write a few paragraphs explaining the overall administration, location, plant or equipment, and supply and distribution requirements of your business. Describe your contingency plans for occasions when suppliers or distributors let you down. Find a map of the location of your business premises to include in appendices. Check with the local authority about any possible requirements regarding premises, noise, neighbours and the environment and obtain any paperwork necessary. Check the insurance situation for any premises you will be using. Check the contract of any suppliers and distributors. If possible, work out a CPA for the main process. Estimate costs for supply, delivery, setting-up costs for plant and premises, and ongoing costs for leasing or renting premises, heating and light.

Summary

Efficient operation of your business is a key component of success. In your business plan you need to explain where your business will be located, what machinery or plant you have or need to obtain, what storage facilities you need, how the production process works, how delivery will be arranged, what hours you will operate and how the product or service will be made available to the customer.

08

explaining the finances

In this chapter you will learn:

- why the finances are important
- how to produce a cash flow forecast
- how to produce a balance sheet
- how to produce a profit and loss forecast
- how to do some further calculations

The key section in your business plan will be the financial statement. In it you will demonstrate the viability of your business over several years. You need to show that you have control of the finance and that you are aware of potential problems and have plans to deal with them. It is possible to produce the financial figures yourself or you can employ an accountant to do so. This chapter explains why it is important to get this section right, what you need to include and how to prepare a basic statement.

Producing the financial statements

To run a business you need at least a basic understanding of accounts. You need to produce the financial statements yourself, if possible. There are many places, including banks, from which you can get business plan templates (including the financial sections) to complete yourself. You can also buy software packages that will enable you to produce a financial statement (see Taking it Further). This chapter will help you complete basic forms. There are many computer accounting packages to help you. If you are uncertain about any details of the accounts, employ an accountant to deal with these and draw up the final version. The cost of his or her services will be amply repaid by an accurately completed financial statement that will be in a form acceptable to any potential investors or grant awarders. A good accountant is worth paying for because they will save you time and money and produce accounts that you can be confident will fulfil any regulatory requirements. However, using an accountant does not take all the responsibility from you. You must make sure that you understand the accounts and can answer questions about them.

Debit and credit

To draw up your financial statements you will need to record things clearly. This can strike fear into many people, but it is really quite simple. Instead of putting the income and expenditure in one column, put them in two. One column will show what comes into the business and the other column will show what goes out. For example, in the cash flow statement you will show what money comes in and goes out of the business and the balance sheet shows columns of assets and debts. You will see how this is done in the examples later in this chapter.

Keeping your business accounts

The financial statements that go into your business plan are not the end of your accounting commitments. Whether you have an existing business or are starting one, you need to have an accounting system in place. A good accounting system is necessary so that you know exactly where the money goes and have the figures available for any VAT queries. You can identify debtors and spot employee malpractice. Accurate and up-to-date accounts also give you and your managers a guide against which planning can take place. If you do not feel confident about handling accounting, or your business expands or is large, then you can employ a bookkeeper or accountant.

Doing it yourself – useful products

There are a number of useful places you can go to get help with completing your financial statements. First of all, most of the major clearing banks will be able to provide you with basic business plan forms which will include financial statements for you to complete. Next, there are websites from which you can download financial statement forms and which will give you guidance about completing them. There are books like this one to give you guidance. Finally, there are a number of software packages for both PCs and Macs which will take you through the steps of completing a cash flow statement or profit and loss account, or indeed any number of other financial statements. Details of these with contact details are at the end of this book in Taking it Further.

Why the finances are important

The financial section of your business plan is where you explain how and why your business will be financially successful. You need to be able to explain how much money you need (or will need) and where you will get it from. Your financial requirements should be set out in a financial needs statement. You need to explain your present and expected financial position and future needs. Any potential investor will ask a number of basic questions to which you must have the answers. These will include:

1 Will your business make a profit?
2 Will you be able to pay all your bills?
3 Have you got any existing financial resources?
4 Do you need a loan? Will you be able to repay it and, if so, how long will it take you?

5 What will it cost to operate the business?
6 Have you dealt with any necessary licences, permits, insurance, etc.?
7 Do your financial statements provide a complete picture of your present financial situation and future financial income and expenditure?

You need to set out clearly the following:

- how much money and other assets your business already has, including any personal assets
- how much money you need (the costs of starting your business or implementing a business idea)
- what it will be used for
- where you will get the money from
- what kind of financial help you want
- how you will pay back any loans
- what investors might expect from the business

The information you need

Before you start to complete any financial statement you need to research the basic financial situation of your business. Your financial statements will be a good indication of how your business will operate financially. But it is only that – an indication. Therefore, the better the research you do to underpin the statements, the more accurate they will be.

You need to know exactly what your present financial situation is regarding the business and to record or estimate based on sound evidence the following facts:

- total sales value of your goods or services
- seasonal trends or other trends that will affect sales
- total monthly sales (and quarterly, yearly)
- credit terms you have already negotiated or expect to get
- monthly cash flow
- details of any additional income, e.g. personal loans
- production and/or sales costs
- administration costs (often overlooked by small businesses – photocopying and stamps cost money!)
- details of any additional costs
- publicity costs
- pricing systems
- advance orders

To back up your statement about how much money you need and where it will be spent you need to provide evidence. This can be done by producing a cash flow forecast and a profit and loss forecast as well as a balance sheet. These are explained later in this chapter.

Be realistic

Some figures you will have already; others you will have to estimate. It is important not to over or underestimate the figures. If you already have some advance orders or bookings you can base your estimates on these. Otherwise you will need to do some market research to find out what realistically the figures might be. Any estimated figures should be realistic, believable and achievable.

You will need to provide evidence that your figures are possible. Support sales projections with sales information from similar businesses, previous sales records (if any), details of any firm orders already received and information about how much your target market generates.

Be honest and accurate

It should go without saying that you should be honest and accurate when compiling your financial statements. Do not exaggerate forecasts or omit figures that you think might not be well received. Your readers need to know exactly where the business stands financially.

What financial statements do you need?

To back up your statement about how much money you need and where it will be spent you need to provide evidence. To provide evidence of your financial needs and your business's expectations you must produce at least three basic financial documents:

1 cash flow forecast
2 balance sheet
3 profit and loss forecast

BUSINESS PLAN TIP
Look at examples of financial statements in business plans. See the websites listed in Taking it Further.

What the statements mean

Each of these types of financial statement provides a particular kind of financial information. Together they will show anyone interested in the viability of your business how financially efficient and secure it is likely to be.

Cash flow forecast

Any potential investors or lenders will need to know whether your business is likely to survive on a monthly basis. The cash flow forecast tells you where your business will go financially over the next 12-month period. It is based on estimates backed by research for a new business. The cash flow forecast shows how your business will operate financially over time and therefore whether you will be able to pay creditors. It should provide enough information to indicate how the business will survive.

> **Cash** – the amount of money that goes into and out of your business.
> **Profit** – the surplus of income over expenditure.

Balance sheet

This provides a snapshot of your business. It shows what the value of your business is now if you are already trading. If you will be starting a new business then you will have to estimate the figures to show what your business will be like under certain conditions in the future. Generally a balance sheet is calculated for the end of a financial year. It provides an overall view of your financial situation and business at a specific time, usually at the end of a year. It shows what your business's debts are and what your business is owed. It is a complete picture of your business's assets and liabilities.

Profit and loss forecast

This simply means a forecast of whether your business will make a profit or loss for a specific period. Your figures should show the results monthly for at least one year and quarterly for two more. Farther ahead than that and the forecast becomes too inaccurate to be useful. Also, you would expect to reassess your calculations in the light of actual business experience after about three years. It is important to recognize that cash and profit are not the same thing in business terms. Most banks or financial institutions can provide profit and loss forms for you to complete.

Existing businesses will also be expected to provide cash flow and profit and loss statements based on existing figures. As the cash flow statement is the most important of these three statements we shall start with that.

Cash flow forecast

This is a record of the amount of money that you expect to come into the business for each period, say weekly, monthly, quarterly or annually, and what you expect the business to pay out. At the end of the period you should be able to calculate what the closing balance at the bank will be.

Basically, you need to show that you will be managing your cash flow efficiently so that the business will survive. The cash flow statement will show the effect on your bank balance over time and whether you are likely to be able to pay your creditors. You need to show what money will be generated by the business, the cash inflow, and what the business expenditure will be, the cash outflow.

Bear in mind that if you are starting a new business you need to allow for short-term expenditure on setting-up costs such as equipment, computers and stocks. You will also almost certainly experience a delay in payments from debtors which at the start may mean that your receipts might not cover your costs. You need a cash flow forecast to see the timing for payments and income and how they will affect each other. It will tell you and your readers when cash will arrive and when you will have to pay bills and therefore when money will leave your account.

You will also need to include any advance orders. It is often the case that businesses just starting up attract orders before the capital is there. You will need to show that you can fulfil these orders and what the costs will be of doing so.

Cash inflow – what you generate by selling your product or service.
Cash outflow – what you spend and what you owe.

Cash inflow is what you receive from sales, loans and investments. Cash outflow might include:

- materials
- labour
- equipment

- rent/rates/taxes
- marketing
- interest on loans and other repayments
- VAT if charged
- payment to professional advisors

The cash flow should show:

- how different seasons or other regular changes will affect your trading
- forecasts of monthly sales
- cash receipts
- total cash inflow
- cost of production of goods or setting-up of services
- regular interest payments
- other expenses
- opening and closing cash balances
- any loans needed

Your net cash flow therefore equals your total monthly receipts minus your total monthly payments. To get the bank balance you add or subtract the final amount from the opening balance. It is standard practice to put minus amounts in brackets.

A sample cash flow statement is shown on page 117. You might need to add or omit items depending on the business. For each month you must include cash receipts for that month.

Sales forecasting

To produce a cash flow forecast you need to be able to estimate what your future sales will be. You also need to be able to explain how you reached the figures you include in the forecast. You can do this by straightforward mathematical means. You can either use a forecast based on annual sales or a Moving Annual Total (MAT) method that uses the previous year's monthly sales figures to project sales. Because you need to take variables such as product, marketing and seasonal changes and other possible external changes into account, this is best calculated in a business software program (see Taking it Further). You can start by recording or estimating a year's monthly sales figures.

BUSINESS PLAN TIP
Make a list of all your (potential) outgoings and group them into broader categories afterwards.

Your business [legal name]
Cash flow forecast for the year ending XX

	JANUARY	FEBRUARY	MARCH
Opening cash balance			
MONEY RECEIVED			
Cash from sales/service			
Cash from receivables collected			
Loan proceeds			
Personal investment			
Sales of assets			
Other specified receipts			
Total receipts			
MONEY PAID OUT			
Accounts payable			
Supplies			
Rent			
Utilities			
Purchase fixed assets			
Insurance			
Professional fees			
Marketing			
Wages			
Salaries			
Long term debt repayments			
Taxes			
Other specified money paid out			
Total monies paid out			
SURPLUS (DEFICIT)			

Figure 4: cash flow forecast

Things to remember

Be careful to record sales made on credit in the month in which the business will actually receive the cash. You will need to estimate the percentage of sales made by cash and credit. If you give credit lasting different lengths of time (for example, 30 or 60 days) make sure you estimate the percentages of credit sales for each period. In the same way, record the amounts payable according to when your suppliers demand payment, which might be different for different suppliers. Only record the due figure in the month for which you actually pay it.

You might find that you run at a loss until your business gets established. In which case a summary of your cash flow would look like the chart below.

	Month 1	Month 2	Month 3	Month 4
balance at start of month	£0	(£2500)	(£3000)	£1000
cash from sales	£0	£0	£4500	£4500
purchase of stock	(£2000)	£0	£0	(£2000)
overheads	(£500)	(£500)	(£500)	(£1500)
monthly balance	(£2500)	(£3000)	£1000	£2000

example cash flow overview

> **Overheads**
> Your overheads will be:
> • wages/salaries
> • premises
> • electricity, gas
> • expenses
> • service levels to other parts of the business (if applicable)

This shows you how a cash flow statement works but you will usually need to provide much more information than this. To support your cash flow statement include copies of any evidence you can provide, such as payment notes and receipts or orders.

Improving your cash flow

By producing a cash flow statement you can see whether your business is likely to generate cash (and therefore encourage investors to lend you their money). It will also act as a guide once you start trading so that you can see where and when you are likely to be in financial difficulties. Existing businesses are likely to be able to produce a satisfactory cash flow forecast based on how the business is already operating. For new businesses maintaining an efficient cash flow is one of the hardest things to do and is a common cause of failure. Although you will not need to go into detail about how you will improve your cash flow in your business plan, there are a number of ways you can make improvements:

1 Send invoices as soon as possible.
2 Don't build up large amounts of money in your business account. Transfer anything above a necessary minimum of money to a deposit account. Deposit receipts daily.
3 Deal with problems promptly and courteously to encourage customers not to withhold payment.
4 Offer customers incentives to pay quickly.
5 Pay your own bills by instalments, if possible.
6 Negotiate better credit and discount terms with your main suppliers.
7 Keep stock or raw materials to the minimum necessary.
8 Introduce performance related pay.
9 Where it would be cheaper to do so, lease equipment rather than buy it.
10 Don't be afraid to change your credit supplier to one who can offer it at lower cost.
11 Don't give credit unless you are convinced customers can pay. If so, charge more.
12 Don't let overdue accounts mount up. Don't hesitate to use legal action, if necessary.
13 Record all phone calls, quotes and estimates to eliminate mistakes in bills.
14 If you don't feel confident about dealing with bills, use factors but be aware of the cost and inconvenience.

Balance sheet

What you include in your balance sheet will depend on what kind of business you have or intend to have. There are different ways to present a balance sheet. A sample balance sheet showing one way is shown below. The balance sheet uses double-entry bookkeeping. The date on the sheet should be the date it was prepared and it should be prepared at the close of business on that day. If you are starting a new business the balance sheet will show an estimated forecast.

Your business [legal name]
Balance sheet as of [date prepared]

ASSETS

<u>Current assets</u>
Cash	£XXX	
Debtors	£XXX	
Merchandise inventory	£XXX	
Office supplies	£XXX	
Stock (store supplies)	£XXX	
Prepaid insurance	£XXX	
Total current assets		£XXX

<u>Plant and equipment</u>
Office equipment	£XXX		
Less depreciation		£XXX	
Store equipment	£XXX		
Less depreciation		£XXX	
Buildings	£XXX		
Less depreciation		£XXX	
Land	£XXX		
Less depreciation		£XXX	
Total plant and equipment			£XXX
Total assets			<u>£XXX</u>

LIABILITIES

<u>Current liabilities</u>
Creditors	£XXX	
Accrued wages	£XXX	
Tax	£XXX	
Total liabilities		<u>£XXX</u>

<u>Owners' equity (Proprietor or partners)</u>
John X, capital	£XXX	
Sally Y, capital	£XXX	
Retained profits/earnings	£XXX	
Total liabilities and owners' equity		<u>£XXX</u>

Figure 5: balance sheet

The balance sheet should be divided into two parts:

1 assets – all the money the business has or is owed and the value of stock, etc.
2 liabilities – what the business owes (including owners' equity), and how much you and partners or shareholders, if relevant, put into the business

The assets and liabilities must be equal, that is they must be 'balanced'. If your business does not include all the items in the example, you can exclude them. On the other hand, if you have other means of income or liabilities not mentioned these should be included. For example, if you already have a bank loan or a grant the cash received as a result should be recorded under current assets.

Assets – the business's economic resources.
Liabilities – what the business owes to other people.

Things to remember

List assets in order of:

* current assets
* long-term investments, e.g. stocks
* plant and equipment – with depreciation, if relevant
* intangible assets, e.g. patent, trademark
* other assets

Then total your assets.

List liabilities in order of:
* current liabilities – due within 12 months
* long-term liabilities – due beyond 12 months
* other liabilities

Then total your liabilities.

Record your owners' liabilities (net worth) and then subtract your total liabilities from your total assets.

Profit and loss forecast

The other important financial document you need to provide is a profit and loss forecast. This will show how much gross profit you expect to make (total profit) and make allowances for depreciation of goods (if relevant) and taxes.

Your business [legal name]
Year ended XXX

<u>Income (revenue)</u>		£XXX
<u>Cost of goods sold/service</u>		
Inventory (start of year)	£XXX	
Salaries/wages	£XXX	
Materials and supplies	£XXX	
Inventory (end of year)	(£XXX)	
		<u>£XXX</u>
<u>Gross profit</u>		£XXX
<u>Expenses</u>		
Marketing	£XXX	
Depreciation of equipment (if relevant)	£XXX	
Gas/electricity/water	£XXX	
Insurance	£XXX	
Interest and bank charges	£XXX	
Maintenance and repairs	£XXX	
Professional fees (e.g. accountant)	£XXX	
Licence/permits	£XXX	
Salaries/wages etc.	£XXX	
Office supplies	£XXX	
Telephone	£XXX	
Vehicle and travel expenses	£XXX	
Loan payments	£XXX	
Net income before taxes		<u>£XXX</u>
Less income taxes		<u>£XXX</u>
Net income		<u>£XXX</u>

Figure 6: profit and loss forecast

The way you set out a profit and loss forecast will depend on the type of business you have or intend to set up. Find out from your bank or a business advisor which format best suits your business. You also need to find out what a similar business would include in costs which directly relate to sales. Also, do not try to estimate future tax bills. If you think you need to include this in the account, ask an accountant to estimate them for you.

A profit and loss forecast is sometimes also called an income statement. Some of the items may not be relevant to your business; if so, omit them.

Depreciation

This applies to plant and equipment that you own and must be calculated for and included in your profit and loss forecast. There are various methods of calculating depreciation and you should take advice from an accountant about which method you should use. However, for the purposes of your plan a basic calculation can be made to get a monthly depreciation figure.

$$\text{depreciation} = \frac{\text{purchase cost}}{\text{years to be used}} \times \frac{1}{12}$$

The importance of calculating depreciation can be seen by using a business vehicle, a van, as an example. The cost of the van itself, repairs and maintenance would be recorded in your cash flow statement in the month in which they occur. These costs will be part of the ongoing costs of the business over the 12-month period of the statement. The estimated depreciation of the van, on the other hand, will be recorded in the profit and loss account because it will be part of the calculation of how much profit the business is making.

> **BUSINESS PLAN TIP**
> Ask other people how long their plant or equipment typically lasted so that you can estimate depreciation for your own plant and equipment.

Things to remember

Note what the various items in a profit and loss statement should include:

- revenue – income from goods and sales after deducting expenses
- cost of goods sold/service – what it actually costs to make your goods/deliver your service, including payments to subcontractors
- gross profit – revenue minus cost of goods sold
- expenses – these will vary depending on the type of business; consult your tax office or accountant for advice

- net income before tax – gross profit minus expenses
- less income tax – tax rate multiplied by net income before taxes (e.g. 33% × £15,000)
- net income – net income before tax minus income tax

You should enter the figures exclusive of VAT. Also in this statement you should record income from sales in the month when the sales are made, not when the money is received.

When forecasting sales, allow for a steady build-up during the initial period as well as any seasonal or other influences. If the business is already operating, include all completed work invoiced even if it has not been paid for yet.

Other calculations

You need to make your financial statements as convincing as possible so there are other figures that you can include to back up your plan.

Start-up costs

A new business should provide a breakdown of all costs associated specifically with starting the business. This should include everything that needs to be in place before the business can start operating. Present this as a simple summary.

Break-even analysis

Lenders and investors like to know at what point your business will break even and therefore when it will start to make a profit. A break-even analysis should be included in your plan. This shows when a new business or project reaches its break-even point, after which it starts to make a clear profit. The break-even point is where the total amount of income from sales covers the cost of producing or buying a product and all other related operating costs. To find out how many products or service appointments you have to sell to break even, you need to:

1 work out the profit for each unit (sales price minus production buying price)
2 divide operating costs by profit per unit

For example, if it costs you £2 to make a widget and you sell it for £5, your profit would be £3 per unit. If your fixed operating costs are £60, your break-even point would be £60 divided by £3, in other words you would need to sell 20 widgets to break even. Every widget you sold after that would start making you a profit.

You can draw a chart to show the break-even point in your business using the sales and operating figures from your cash flow forecast. Record your expected costs over expected sales from the start of the business for the duration of the plan. At the start you would expect costs to be greater than sales income, but this changes as sales increase. Figure 7 shows the break-even point where the two lines cross on the graph.

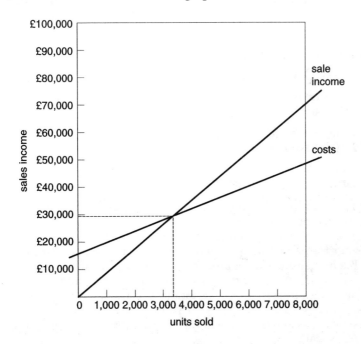

Figure 7: example break-even analysis graph

Gross profit margin

This is your budgeted gross profit (total sales minus total direct costs) divided by total sales and multiplied by 100. It is represented as a percentage.

$$\text{gross profit margin (\%)} = \frac{\text{gross profit}}{\text{sales}} \times 100$$

Things to note

When preparing your profit and loss statement you need to match periods for income and costs. These should both appear in the period to which they relate to, not the period in which they occur. For example, if you pay two months in advance for supplies, this will be recorded in the period for which it refers, not when it was paid. In the same way, money you receive in advance should be recorded for the period to which it refers, not when you receive it.

When estimating depreciation write off the same amount each year based on the period for which the plant, machinery or equipment are likely to last.

Potential pitfalls

There are two ways in which your financial analysis might cause problems:

1 unrealistic forecasts
2 false assumptions

Unrealistic forecasts

You need to make sure that you do not overestimate the likely returns your business will make. Any investor or lender will want to see a profitable and sustainable return on their money and your forecasts should show that your business will provide this. But be realistic. Do not promise what you are unlikely to provide, otherwise your supporters might back out if expectations are not met. It is difficult not to overestimate, but look around at what your competitors are doing. If you can find annual reports on similar businesses these will give you an idea of what to expect realistically.

False assumptions

It is easy to fall into the trap of making false assumptions. For example, don't assume that because there are 66 million people in Britain you will sell to 20 per cent of them and make a fortune. Or that because everyone drinks water your new water filter will sell to everyone. Basing your forecasts on simplistic assumptions like that will distort the figures and discredit your plan.

Provide evidence

As mentioned at the start of this chapter, you need to provide evidence to support your forecasts. You do not need to go into details in the body of your plan although you should provide references when relevant. In the appendices you should provide notes about how you reached your forecast figures and assumptions, backing them up with research you have done. Include price lists to support your sales forecasts and guaranteed orders when available.

BUSINESS PLAN TIP
Remember to include references to statements from books, journals, newspapers or websites. Use the most up-to-date information as possible to add credibility.

If things go wrong

Just preparing your financial statements and forecasts will not in itself guarantee success, but they will provide a guide as to how you conduct your business. However, readers will also want to know what you will do if your financial situation does not work out as planned. Sit down and think of contingency plans to cover such things as lack of sales, over demand, profit margin too small, no demand, increased competition, operational or managerial problems, and so on. By providing well thought-out alternative solutions you show that you understand the market and your place within it.

Although you must be honest about the potential risks you should aim to foresee any questions that readers might ask. If you present a business plan that claims that your business is risk free it will not be credible. On the other hand you must show that you are ready for any risks as they occur. Your proposed solutions should show that the problem is not large and that it would not damage your business. You should explain how you would deal with the problem and the likely outcome of your solutions.

Test
(See page 199 for answers.)

1 What three financial documents must you include in your business plan?
2 What does cash inflow mean?
3 How do you record a deficit in a financial statement?
4 What method of accounting should you use?
5 What are the three parts to a balance sheet?
6 Name the two potential pitfalls of preparing financial statements.
7 What is break-even analysis?

Plan preparation

The amount of financial information that you put into the plan will depend on how large and how complex your business is. It also depends on whether you are already trading. If you are trading you will have more figures available. Your intended audience will also influence how much information about your finances you include. If you are producing the plan to ask for financial aid, then you will need as much detailed financial information as you can produce. In the body of the plan you will put summaries of what your financial documents tell you. In the appendices you will put the financial details themselves. Not all the detailed information will go in the body of your plan. The forecasts and evidence will be placed in the appendices along with any evidence you have supporting the figures and your assumptions. In the body of the plan concentrate on describing the main assumptions and include a section about your assumptions next to a summary of the forecasts. Explain all the important points and include a summary of your trading. Remember that the summary has to be believable.

Put your forecast figures next to the figures that show your trading history (if relevant). You should include:

- profit and loss forecast
- balance sheet (if relevant)
- cash flow forecast
- breakdown of start-up costs
- break-even analysis

What you are trying to show is your trading result (or intended trading result).

Summary

The financial statements included in your plan are vital to the success of your presentation. They will indicate to potential lenders or investors the financial viability of your business and your prospects of long-term success. The basic documents you should include are a cash flow forecast, balance sheet and profit and loss forecast. Banks and accountants can help you. There are also software packages to make the process easier.

09

**deciding the
timetable**

In this chapter you will learn:

- how to choose a timescale for business forecasts
- how to choose a timescale for plan preparation
- how to approach preparing your plan
- how to implement your business plan

There are three kinds of timetable that you need to consider. The first is what length of time should your business forecasts cover. The second is how long you will need to prepare the business plan. The third is how long you will need to implement your plan. The first is quickly answered and depends on the type of your business. The second also depends on what kind of business you will be running, but also on how much information you already have and how much you need to complete the plan. The third will depend on the nature of your business and how quickly it can be put into operation. This chapter will explain the timescale for each of these considerations.

Timetable for forecasts

You need to be clear about your objectives. All businesses should look ahead in the short, medium and long term. Your plan should demonstrate that you know where your business will be going in the future and that you are prepared for changes and have thought about how it will be operating both practically and financially for several years ahead.

Generally you can think of objectives as:

1 short-term – the first year
2 medium-term – the next two years
3 long-term – more than three years

Getting the forecast period right can be tricky. You shouldn't present forecasts, either financial or setting-up, that are too brief and therefore do not take into account likely changes in your business. Nor do you want to project forecasts so far ahead that the timing and figures become meaningless and the numbers you have calculated have changed so much that you are simply guessing.

At least a year

Any business plan that includes forecasts for less than a year is simply not going to convince readers. You need to persuade them that your business will last at least that long and that you have a clear idea about how it will progress both financially and operationally during that time. On the other hand, you do not need to go into minute day-to-day detail. So what is a reasonable time scale to use for your plan?

Choosing a timescale

For most business you will need to provide forecasts for not only the first year but for several years after that. The first year's forecast will be detailed but the later years can be outlines. How many subsequent years will depend on the size of your business. For small businesses it will be appropriate to provide forecasts for two years subsequent to the first (three years in all); larger businesses might provide four outline years of forecasts (five years in all). Any forecasts that try to look ahead further than five years are probably in the realms of fantasy. Business life changes so rapidly nowadays that it is difficult to predict anything beyond a few years ahead with any certainty.

The ideal timescale

An ideal timescale for the forecasts would be:

- one year detailed PLUS two years outline (small business)
- one year detailed PLUS four years outline (large business)

How long for your business?

You might have difficulty in deciding whether you need a three- or five-year plan. Think about the size of your business and how long it will take to set up. If it is a small business and will be quick to set up, then provide a three-year plan. If you want a large business or it will take some time before the business is running at full strength, then provide a five-year plan. You also need to take your staff into account. If there is only you or one or two partners, then you might be able to provide a longer-term plan than if your business will have lots of staff who change frequently and on whose commitment you cannot always rely.

> **BUSINESS PLAN TIP**
> If in doubt, choose the three-year plan.

Timescale for preparing the plan

The only sure thing about deciding how long you need to prepare your business plan is that it will take longer than you think. If you have been making notes and following the guidance in the previous chapters you will have a lot of research already completed. However, there will be more that you need depending on the type of business and whether there is specific information in business plan forms produced by your potential lenders or investors that you need to include.

You need to take into account a number of things before you decide on the timing:

- how much information you already have
- how much information you need to collect
- where you will get the information from
- who you will ask to help you
- whether you need to consult partners or employees
- whether you will be writing the plan yourself or asking someone to help you

Using a timetable

Keep yourself on track by drawing up a timetable for completion of your business plan. Break down your tasks into smaller steps – for example, desk research on competitors, writing paragraphs on operations, contacting trade organizations. When you make a timetable don't put it in a drawer and forget it. You need to look at it frequently while you are gathering the information and writing the plan so that you keep on track. Make sure that you do everything that is required of you to complete the plan, particularly if you are using a form provided by the financial or other organization you are targeting. Unless you are certain that a section is unnecessary, complete it.

Before you start

Don't just plunge into creating your timetable. Make sure that you understand what you need before you start. Read any documentation you are to complete so that you are clear what is required of you. If in any doubt, contact the organization you are targeting, whether a bank, investment house or other, and *ask*. Don't guess. You need to know exactly what is needed.

Also, if you intend to use outside help to create or write up your plan make sure that you have booked them well in advance. They will need adequate time to do their work.

Questionnaire

Before you make your timetable ask yourself these questions:

1 Is there a deadline for completing my plan?
2 What do I need to find out?
3 Who do I need to speak to?
4 Which organizations should I contact?
5 Are there any regulations with which I must comply?
6 Am I a member of all relevant organizations and are my memberships up-to-date?
7 Are there libraries, websites, books or journals I need to consult?
8 Do I need to do any field research?
9 Are there any people who can give me practical help with my plan?
10 Are there any costs involved with the research?

Once you have decided who you need to see and what you need to find out you can sit down and write a rough timetable of how much each stage will take. Don't forget to include the actual writing-up time. Bearing in mind any deadline you have been given, start from when you hope to present your plan and work backwards. Allow slightly more time than you think you need – something will always delay you. A straightforward plan for a small business might take three to six months to produce; a larger or more complicated business might take longer. However, these times will depend on how complicated your business is and how much time you can spend on it.

Divide your plan

As suggested earlier in this chapter, it will help you to plan your time if you break down what you need to do into smaller steps. If you have done the exercises in this book so far, you will already have draft paragraphs for all the main sections of your plan. You will need to check these in the light of any new research and double-check any figures. You can use the timetable below as a check on progress. If you have not yet started, begin at the first stage. Typical steps in your timetable might be:

Stage one

- note what information you already have, including rough financial estimates
- decide what information you need

- decide which people and organizations to contact
- draw up a timetable and list of contacts
- do desk research
- decide whether and what field research you need to do
- making preliminary decisions

Stage two

- contact experts
- contact organizations
- write drafts of non-financial sections

Stage three

- draw up list of managers
- collect CVs, references, qualifications, certificates, etc.
- research product or service, business services, location
- research distribution, suppliers
- rewrite drafts of non-financial sections

Stage four

- collate financial estimates
- check financial requirements
- work out the numbers
- draft financial forecasts
- redraft forecasts according to research

Stage five

- collate drafts
- check drafts and write up each section
- make any changes according to latest research
- check plan for grammatical and spelling mistakes
- get someone else to read plan
- collate plan and present it

Obviously this timetable will not suit everyone or every business. If your needs are different you can adapt it, but make sure that you cover each stage of the plan.

Another way of approaching it is to divide the timetable for creating the plan into broad sections and then break these down into more detailed stages.

1 find out what you need to put in the plan
2 list every person and organization you need to contact
3 list the separate parts
4 break each part down into three or four stages

5   include a final stage for writing the plan
6   estimate how long each stage will take
7   work through the timetable

BUSINESS PLAN TIP
Use your computer's calendar (e.g. Microsoft Outlook) to help you plan your timetable.

Using checklists

To help you keep on track use checklists to help you. List all the people, information, organizations and so on that you need to deal with. Next to each item on the list write down *how* you are going to get the information. Set a target date for talking to, meeting or contacting people you need to get information from and for obtaining information for other sources. When you have got the information write the completion date beside the item. This will quickly tell you whether you are running slowly and, if so, by roughly how much and you can then adjust your timetable accordingly. When all the information is assembled you can complete the writing-up of your plan (this is covered in detail in the following chapter).

BUSINESS PLAN TIP
Carry a notebook and a copy of your timetable everywhere. You can complete some tasks in any short periods of free time you get.

Implementing the plan

Once your plan has achieved its purpose of obtaining outside help, if relevant, you need it to help you start the business. The timetable of forecasting within it will give you an idea of how long you need to get started.

It is possible to set up small businesses very quickly, especially if you will be operating on your own and already have the expertise required. Generally, you will need time to get things set up if you are starting from scratch. If you are setting up a business as part of a franchise you will get help from the franchisers and they will be able to provide guidance on any problems you are experiencing and the timescale you need to allow.

For most businesses you need to allow time for a number of things:

- obtaining the finance
- complying with any legalities
- buying or leasing premises
- obtaining plant/machinery/equipment
- hiring staff and training them (if necessary)
- producing product or organizing service
- getting product or service to first customers
- getting paid
- reaching break-even point

Obtaining the finance

How long this will take will depend on the type of finance you need and who will be providing it. You need to allow time for a decision to be made and for the lender, investor or grant provider to arrange for the money to reach you. They should be able to give you an idea of how long it will take them to reach a decision.

Sorting out legalities

Once you have the financial situation settled you can sort out any legalities. These might be licensing, health and safety and fire certificates, and so on. The regulatory bodies will be able to give you some idea of how long it will take to inspect and certificate (always longer than you think or would like). If you are hoping to renovate or buy premises and planning permission or other permissions for building (building regulations or listed building consent) will be required, then you must allow much longer. The council will tell you how long the process should take. You then need to allow time for the work to be done before you can move your offices or production process into the building. If this is going to take longer than you would like, you should be thinking about temporary accommodation for your business while permissions are obtained and work is going on.

Obtaining premises

You might have premises in mind but have not already obtained them. The time to do so is when you have the finances confirmed. As well as your preferred premises, you should also think of several alternatives. The usual time for buying once a sale is agreed is six weeks, although it can sometimes be done more quickly. If you are waiting in a buying chain then you cannot accurately predict the time it will take. Renting premises will be quicker assuming suitable premises are available, and this might be a sensible option as it will give you time to buy premises. If you are working from home you can use the time waiting for confirmation of your financial status to check whether there are any mortgage or council regulations you need to comply with. If there are and you cannot satisfy these, you will have to look for alternative premises.

Obtaining plant/machinery/equipment

If you are offering a personal service such as aromatherapy or work from home then you might already have the equipment you need. Or you might be offering a class, in which case your pupils might provide their own equipment while you provide tuition and premises. For larger businesses, however, you will need the basics to produce the product or provide the service.

While you are waiting for a decision about financial aid you should be searching for suppliers of necessary plant and machinery or any other equipment you need. Check out the firms' prices and their guarantees and whether they repair on your premises. Find out whether hiring would be more cost-effective. If your business will be small and the equipment common, you might be able to borrow it from friends or relatives for a short period until you can afford buy or lease your own.

Hiring staff

If you are going to employ other people you need to sort out how to deal with their National Insurance, tax, contracts of employment and other necessary details. Contact the tax office for advice while you are waiting for the financial aspects of your business to be completed.

Training staff

If your employees will need training before they can start work you need to find out how much this will cost and where it can be done, if you are not training them on the job. Preferably use training schemes that end with a recognized qualification or skill certification. This reassures you that your staff are qualified to a certain standard and enables them to build on their skills at a later date.

Producing product or setting up service

It will take time to produce your first batch of products or set up a service so that it can be delivered to customers. This will involve not only manufacturing or organizing what you will be selling, but arranging supply, delivery, packaging, publicity and all the other things that go into getting a business off the ground. In your plan you should have already stated how long you think this start-up phase will take.

Getting product or service to first customers

The final timescale you need to take into account is the time it will take to get your product or service to your first customers. This is part of the delivery process mentioned above.

Getting paid

It might be weeks or months before you get money coming into your business. The summary of your cash flow forecast will enable you to work out how long this will take and therefore how much time you need for financial back-up.

Reaching break-even point

After doing a simple break-even analysis (as shown in Chapter 8) you will see how many units or service appointments you have to sell to break even. This, together with your cash flow forecast, will tell you how long it will take you to reach break-even point.

Test
(See page 199 for answers.)
1 What three plan timescales do you need to be aware of?
2 What is the minimum period a business plan should cover?
3 How many years should a plan for a large business cover?
4 How do you make a timetable manageable?
5 What must you sort out before you implement the plan?

Plan preparation

Make a rough estimate of what you need to do to complete the following and then you can start to create a timetable:

- collect all the information you need – in-house and outside sources
- decide who you need to talk to – people in similar businesses, experts, officials, investors, lenders, grant providers, potential customers
- if you need information from other areas of your business, contact suppliers, long-term customers, partners, employees
- contact the relevant agencies to find out what the requirements are for dealing with tax, insurance, VAT, etc.
- obtain regulatory information for employees and place of work and check certificates are up-to-date – health and safety, discrimination, maternity leave, etc.
- ensure that your memberships of professional or trade organizations are up-to-date

Summary

There are three timescales to consider – what period your plan should cover, how long it will take to prepare the plan, and how long it will take to implement it. These will depend on the size and complexity of your business. The plan should cover between three and five years of operation. Preparation should be broken down into smaller stages. You can take steps to implement the plan before you have confirmation of its acceptance.

10

writing the plan

In this chapter you will learn:

- how to format a business plan
- how to proof-read your plan
- the basics of business plan content
- how to write an executive summary
- how to write the business plan sections

By reading the previous chapters you now have enough information to complete your business plan. Allow plenty of time for writing it – it will take longer than you think. This chapter tells you how to set out your plan, what information you need to put into the plan and how long it should be. An example of a completed business plan is included at the end of the book.

Business plan software

There are software programs available that will enable you to complete your business plan on your computer. You can also download business plan forms and sample business plans from the internet. Some firms that sell business plan software and some internet sites that offer free business plan forms are listed in the Taking it Further section. Remember that the plans will be generic so be prepared to alter the sample forms and plans to suit your own business. If you are still uncertain about your ability to write the plan you can employ a business plan writer to do it for you. Give all your research to them and let them produce the final document, but make sure you understand what they have written and can answer questions on it.

Privacy

Most plans will not need to consider the wider implications of privacy and confidentiality, but if your plan is particularly sensitive you might need to ask recipients to sign confidentiality agreements. You can include a sentence or two in the front of the plan binding the readers to confidentiality or you can choose to omit the information that might cause problems. However, this might not be possible if the information is vital to the reader's understanding of the business. Also, if you are including names and contact details of people who might wish to preserve their privacy you might need their permission to do so. If you are in any doubt about whether you need to bind readers to confidentiality, consult a solicitor.

Formatting the plan

When you start to write your plan you need to keep in mind some basic rules about how to write it and set it out. The better looking and easier to read your plan is the more receptive readers will be.

That does not mean using lots of fancy typefaces and irrelevant pictures but keeping everything clean and clear.

Use plenty of headings and subheadings to guide your readers and use bullet points and numbered lists where relevant.

Keep it short and simple (KISS)

The more direct version of this mnemonic is 'Keep it simple, stupid!' Remember that you want your plan to be clear and readable. Keep your plan as concise as possible while including all the necessary information. Write it in the third person – do not write 'I' or 'me'; instead use 'the business will . . .'. Make sure that your writing is straightforward and to the point. Don't use long words or jargon. Only use business or trade specific words if absolutely necessary to explain how your business works. You need to ensure that potential investors or lenders will be able to understand exactly what your business will do and what you hope for financially. You do not want to leave room for any misunderstandings. Once you have written your plan, check it through for spelling and grammar mistakes. *Always* read it on a paper copy, not just on a computer screen. It is far too easy to miss mistakes on a screen. Ideally, ask someone else to read it through for mistakes.

Clarity

Clarity is the key point to remember as you write your plan. Your business idea will not have a chance unless anyone who reads it can understand exactly why your business will succeed. One sensible way to get an idea of whether it is clear and easy to read is to ask two or three people to read it who have no connection with your business. Ask them whether they understood the document and whether they found the information was presented in the right order. A good test of whether you have written a clear plan is to ask them to explain to you briefly what your business plan is. If they can't, you need to rewrite it.

Cut out the jargon

A warning here – don't use jargon in your business plan unless it is unavoidable. Most businesses, trades or professions have words, phrases, and initials that are specific to them. These are well understood by people in the same line of work and operate as helpful shorthand within the business. For other people these words can be confusing, misleading or simply irritating. Anyone reading your business plan will want to get straight to the facts and gain a clear understanding of what your business will do and how it will work. So cut out the jargon and use standard language wherever possible. Aim to put down your thoughts clearly and unambiguously.

BUSINESS PLAN TIP
When you have written a section of your business plan give it to someone outside the business to read – a friend, your mother, someone in another line of work. If they don't understand it, ask them what they found difficult and rewrite it.

Check for errors

Nothing will irritate your readers more than a document full of spelling and grammatical mistakes or typos. Don't rely on your computer's spellchecker and grammar checker to sort things out. Mistakes are easy to miss on a screen. Also, your spellchecker might pass words that are spelt correctly but are in the wrong place, such as 'is this the write way to the shops?' The spellchecker can be useful for a basic first check through the document, but make sure that it is set to the correct language. In most cases this will be obvious, but British and American English, for example, have different spellings. If you are not confident that your language skills or editing skills are adequate, hire somebody to copy-edit your document for you.

Proof-reading trick
Print out a copy of your plan and then read it backwards, starting each page from the bottom and reading towards the top. By looking at it from this different point of view, mistakes will stand out more clearly.

Check your plan for:
• spelling
• grammar
• clarity
• ease of reading
• length

Paper and printing

Do not get too fancy with layout and fonts. The plan should be produced on white A4 paper. Print on one side only and use single spacing. Use a word processor or get somebody else to word process the document. Use black 12 point font in something easy to read, such as Times New Roman font. Do not keep changing the font's type or size. You can use underlining or bold to emphasize titles and headings. Use numbered and bullet lists for easy reading where applicable. Supporting documents can be photocopied for inclusion unless the institution you are approaching insists on originals. Number all the pages consecutively from the first page after the cover sheet until the end. Ideally, put your name or the name of your business as a header on each page. This can easily be done in a word-processing program, and it will help readers put the pages back in the correct order if the binding comes loose. Put a blank sheet at the end with your name and address on it and put a clear plastic A4 sheet on the front and back, or use plain card covers. You can bind the document in a simple ring binder or get the document bound at a print shop. There are a variety of simple plastic bindings, such as comb binding or slide binding, that will hold the document together. Do not try to be clever with the presentation. Keep the document portrait format and if you include illustrations or diagrams keep them clear and uncluttered (see Taking it Further for a useful book on how to present statistics and diagrams).

How long should it be?

The length of the plan will depend on the type of business, but aim to keep it as short as possible while including all the relevant information. If you produce a plan longer than about 30 pages your readers will fall asleep before they have finished it. On the other hand, if your plan is less than about ten pages long it probably will not contain all the information you need to explain your business. Write the plan to include all the important points but don't add unnecessary details.

Top tips for a well-presented plan
 1 use straightforward jargon-free language
 2 keep paragraphs short
 3 use headings to break up text
 4 include an executive summary

5 use one font throughout (e.g. Times New Roman)
6 include relevant graphs and plans
7 include relevant facts and figures where possible (with references)
8 number the pages throughout
9 put covers on your plan
10 bind the document securely
11 keep the document to a manageable size

Supporting facts and figures

Having worked your way through this book, you will have a lot of information. It is important to keep your writing as succinct as possible but support your arguments with facts and figures wherever possible. Rather that saying, for example, 'There are only a few other companies competing with the proposed business . . .' write, 'This business will have only three competitors, XYZ, ABC, EFG, who occupy 27% of the present market. . .'.

Make sure that you include the reference for any supporting facts and figures. This need only be brief but will show that you are not inventing them. For example, the sentence above might be followed by, in brackets, '(*Economic Times*, Nov. 2003, p.7)'. The reference should be detailed enough so that somebody else could check it, but not so long that it contains irrelevant material. The minimum you need is the name of the source, its date and the page number. If you are quoting somebody's speech, you should give their name, the occasion, for example Northhill Business Conference, and the date they spoke. The more up-to-date your references are, the more convincing they will be to readers.

What goes in your plan?

The contents of your plan will depend on the type of business, but there are certain items that all plans should contain. You need a cover sheet, executive summary, description of your business, an explanation of who runs it, how it operates and its financial situation as well as any further relevant information. So, your plan might contain all or any of the following sections:

1 cover page
2 contents
3 executive summary

4 business profile
5 what you are selling and its USP
6 market
7 marketing plan
8 operations
9 management and organization
10 financial information including financial needs
11 appendices

An alternative way of looking at the contents of your plan is to divide it into the main components. So your plan would contain:

- title page and table of contents
- executive summary and business profile
- marketing plan
- operational plan
- human resources plan
- financial plan
- appendices

The exact contents of your plan will depend on your business and who the plan is aimed at.

Cover sheet/title page

This should have the name of your business, your contact details (name, address, phone number, mobile phone number, fax number, e-mail address, web page address). An existing business with a logo could put this on the cover sheet. If you have any partners their names should be listed here. Also if you need to ensure reader confidentiality, this is the place to state the terms. Sometimes a confidentiality form is placed at the beginning of the document and readers are required to sign it.

Also include the period of time the plan covers, for example one year, three years, etc. Include the date that the plan was prepared so that readers can judge how up-to-date it is.

Contents

This should include a list of all sections of the plan, including appendices, together with the page numbers. You will write this once the plan has been completed to ensure that the contents page records what is in the document. If you prepare it last you can change the order of the contents without having to rewrite the contents page each time.

Executive summary

This section is often omitted but is actually a vital part of the plan. It is so important that readers in a hurry will only read this part of your plan and might judge your entire plan only on the executive summary. If you omit this section your plan will have little chance of success. It tells the reader what you want. Put this up front so the reader understands exactly why you are presenting the plan. You should use it to record the salient points of each section on one side of A4 paper if possible, two at the most. The summary should be a clear but succinct précis of the main points of the plan and your argument supporting it. The executive summary is the part of the plan that will be referred to most often, even by people who have read the entire plan. Many people will only read the summary so you need to ensure that it is well written and interesting. This section will be written last because you will need to know exactly what is written in the body of the plan before you can summarize it.

The executive summary should include a statement of purpose. This should explain briefly what the plan hopes to achieve, that is whether you are applying for a loan, want investment, and are hoping for sponsorship, and so on. Do not forget to explain what you are asking for. This is why you are preparing the plan and it should not be left until last.

The summary should continue by providing brief details of the business as it is now, who will run it, who will pay for what you will sell and how much, your business objectives, the benefits and risks, a summary of the financial forecast and what you want from the reader. Do not forget to state how you expect to attain your business targets. Include a statement about what financial help or resources you want from the reader, how the money will be used and how you will repay it. You need only touch briefly on marketing and the competition in this section and omit any figures unless they are vital. Keep the summary to essential points only. Remember that this is only a summary; you will be expanding on these topics later in the plan.

The executive summary should include:

- the idea – what the business is, who its customers will be, what you will sell, and the USP
- financial needs
- main financial points
- present business position

- major business achievements (if any) – if you are a new business have you won any competitions for your product or service idea?

Description of business/business profile

This section should contain all the necessary information about your business set-up, but as a brief overview. Start by explaining why you started the business. Then follow with a brief description of the industry it will be part of and how your business will fit in. Describe how it will succeed and include any facts and figures that will support this. Describe the structure and management briefly and explain how the product or service will be distributed. Include the legal name and contact details for your business and the legal status of the business. It should list the key staff (including yourself) and any partners, if relevant, and explain where the business will be situated. The business's objectives and mission statement would be stated, that is what the business aims to do and what you want from readers. You should include a history of the business to date if the business is already trading. Although the finances will be discussed in detail later you should explain how much your business expects to earn, what you will use new money for and how you expect to repay it. You should place your business within its industry so you need to explain how it relates to other similar businesses in size, products or services. Explain what your business expects to do and how it expects to earn its money.

Remember that readers might not understand how your type of business works as well as you do. Explain it clearly and do not use industry specific words unless you can't explain technicalities any other way.

> **Mission statement**
> A mission statement is the statement of the aims of your business. If you are writing a business plan for an existing business include information about when you started trading, VAT details and what you have been selling.

What you are selling

This is the place to explain exactly what you will be selling. Is it a product or a service? What is its unique selling point (USP)?

Why do you think it will sell? How far has it been developed? What feedback have you had about it so far? How does it compare with other competing products or services? What demand is there for your product or service? You need to convince the reader that what you sell will be welcome to potential customers. The information for this will come from your research for Chapter 3.

Market

Here you describe who you are selling to – your clients or customers – and how you place your product or service in the prevailing market. Explain the results of any market research and quote facts and figures to back up your choice of potential customers. What particular market will your product or service be part of – for example, retail, industrial, financial, service sector, creative? What segment of the market will you be aiming for? Describe the main market trends and identify where your business will fit in in terms of size, position and segmentation. Will you be competing for the same customers or different ones? How do you know who they are and whether they will be receptive to what you sell? Estimate what your share of the market will be. This is where you explain who your customers will be and why they will love what you sell.

Marketing plan

Having explained who your potential customers are you need to explain how you will inform them of what you have to offer. This is where you describe your marketing plan, that is how you will deal with advertising and publicity, what your pricing policy will be and how you will deal with distribution and selling. Even the smallest and most localized business needs to deal with this even if all you intend to do is advertise by word of mouth. All businesses need to know how they will determine prices and how they will get their product or service to the people who want it. If you have done any test marketing, mention the results here. The market and marketing plan sections might be combined. Use the research you did for Chapter 5 here.

Operations

This should be a précis of your operating system, that is how your business will work on a day-to-day basis. Keep it brief but cover all the main points such as production, premises, materials and suppliers, equipment, staffing, delivery, storage, billing methods and legal and insurance needs. What advantages or disadvantages over your competitors do you have? What premises and equipment will you use? How many personnel do you need to operate the business? You can include a diagram of the system in the appendices, if relevant.

Management and organization

In this section describe the management system of your business. Explain the key management positions and what they require from managers. If you are the sole owner and have no employees, this section will be brief. Even so, you will need to explain how you intend to deal with running the business and what your strengths are. If there will be deficiencies, explain how your management team will overcome them. Identify future management needs and how you expect to fill them. If there will be non-executive directors, partners or other key personnel their roles must be described. If your business is larger, then include a diagram in the appendices of the management of the business as explained in Chapter 6. Name all the managers and explain what skills and expertise each will bring to the business and what role they will play. Their CVs will appear in the appendices.

Financial information

This is the place to explain how your business will operate financially as explained in Chapter 8. You should include information about the start-up budget and costs of any expansion as well as information about pricing and costing. You need to explain what money it already has and how you hope to raise more. Have you invested your own money in the business? Explain how you will survive financially on a personal level while running the business. You should explain how money will be spent and how you hope to use any new money. Back up your arguments with facts and figures. In essence, it is a summary of the cash flow, forecasting and balance sheets that you prepared earlier and which will be placed in the appendices.

Financial needs

This is why you are preparing the plan. You want money so you need to explain how much you want and when, why and how you want it. You also need to explain how you expect to repay the lender or investor. If you are applying, or have applied, for other kinds of financial assistance, mention them here. (If you are not asking for money but some other kind of support such as a donation or loan of property or equipment or the provision of volunteer staff, for example, this is still a financial burden for the provider.) Also explain here what extra benefits the reader will get from helping you. This might not just be financial in the form of profits, for example, but might include such things as publicity, kudos or introduction into a particular industry or market.

Security

This is linked to the previous section and should be included if relevant. You should give details of your assets. If you are putting your house up as security for a loan, for example, you need to record this.

Appendices

The appendices contain all the supporting information for your plan. If there are many pages to go in the appendices, divide them into appropriate sections. Include in the appendices any official or relevant documents that support the plan, such as rent agreements, professional qualifications or copies of advance orders. This is the place to include originals of documents if required by potential lenders or investors. The appendices should also contain any other relevant information, such as your managers' CVs, a location map of your premises, your financial spreadsheets, and so on. The aim is to make sure that the reader will have all the relevant information to hand so that they can make an informed decision.

If your business is already established you might already have orders to fill. Or you might have advance orders for a new business idea if potential customers already like what you offer. In either case details of the orders should be included in the appendices of your business plan so that readers can see that you have customers keen to buy. This is proof that your plan has correctly targeted potential customers and therefore is more likely to be viable.

Supporting documents

The supporting documents you include will depend on the type of business. They might include:

- brief summary of trading history (if relevant)
- orders received (if any)
- official agreements, e.g. partnership, leasing or buying premises, previous loans, vehicle hire, suppliers and distributors contracts
- letters concerning the business
- statutory certificates, e.g. fire safety, liquor licence
- award certificates
- qualification certificates, e.g. degree/trade, professional memberships, attendance at skills courses
- details of patents, trade marks, logos, etc.
- other supporting documents concerning your business
- CVs, qualifications and references for you and your managers
- financial information – balance sheet, cash flow forecasts, profit and loss statement with supporting information
- relevant charts and statistics, e.g. financial trends, break-even point
- location map of business premises
- illustrations of product or service premises
- details of orders already received
- technical descriptions (if relevant)
- brochures and catalogues
- results of market research and other relevant reports

Make sure that each page in the appendices is numbered and is clearly labelled so that its purpose is clear. The contents of the appendices should be included on the contents page of the plan so that they can be quickly and easily referred to as the plan is read.

BUSINESS PLAN TIP

Your computer software package might include templates or links to online templates that can help you with your business plan and presentation as well as running your business, for example balance sheet, break-even analysis, start-up capital estimate. Taking it Further includes links to online business plan templates.

Other items

Having completed your plan, you might decide that you need to include other items to support it that do not fall easily into other categories. For example, you might want to include a CD, DVD, tape, computer disk or video. This might be important if you are proposing a business based on a creative discipline and your product or service can be best explained through multi-media.

Lenders or investors might ask for a copy of your plan on disk as well as a paper copy. If you do include non-paper items like these you need to ensure that they are packaged securely with the plan so that they do not get separated from it and lost. Use a transparent pocket with a flap to store a CD or computer disk, or buy special pages that have pockets to hold such items securely and bind them in with the plan. If you are using cardboard covers, attach a pocket for them securely inside the back cover. A video, tape or DVD can be placed in a transparent zip bag with the plan to keep them together. Any extra item should be included in the contents list with a description of where it is stored so that it can be easily located. Listing the item at the front also ensures that the reader can spot it if it is missing. Another way of including extra items is to put them, together with the plan, into a suitably labelled box file or deep, elastic-secured cardboard folder. Label each item to show it belongs to your plan and make sure that your contact details are on the file, plan and extra items.

> **BUSINESS PLAN TIP**
> Keep a copy of the plan and any extra items. Even in the most organized of cases documents and disks can get lost. If you send your plan by post rather than delivering it by hand, phone a day or two later to make sure it has arrived safely. Have a replacement copy ready to replace a missing one quickly.

Back it up!

You shouldn't need reminding to back up your plan from your computer regularly onto a disk. The disk should be stored in a safe place. Not only will this ensure that the latest version of your plan is safe from computer failure but you can easily run off extra copies even if you do not have access to your own computer.

Don't forget the obvious

The final check you should make is to ensure that all the parts of your plan are present before you post it or hand it in. Look at the contents page and then check through the document. It is easy to miss out a section or a vital paragraph. Have you overlooked something obvious like your contact details or a section about your competitors? Or are the pages in the wrong order? The sections in your plan might be slightly different from the sections suggested in this book, but your plan should cover all those elements even if they are included under different headings or are part of different sections. You might also have extra sections that are specific to your business. Check that they are all included. Do a final check of the spelling and grammar.

Checking supporting data

Don't forget to look at the supporting data you have included. This might be in the text itself or in the form of diagrams, graphs, illustrations, etc. Is all the information there? Is it clearly related to the text? Is numerical information complete and accurate? Is it relevant and does it support your argument? Is it referenced clearly so that the reader can refer to them easily? Check the supporting documents. Is it clear what they are and to which section of the plan they refer? Are they clearly labelled, if necessary, and in the order to which they will be consulted?

Test

(See page 199 for answers.)

1 What does KISS mean?
2 Describe a good proof-reading trick.
3 What is arguably the most important part of your business plan?
4 Should you write in the first or third person?
5 What should you include when quoting facts and figures?
6 Where should supporting documents go?

Plan preparation

When you have finished the plan and before you give or send it on, do a final check. Ask yourself these questions:

1 Are all necessary additional documents included?
2 Are all the pages present?
3 Are the sections in the right order?
4 Is the information presented in the correct order?
5 Is the spelling and grammar correct?
6 Are the diagrams and charts relevant and clear?
7 Are there clear headings?

8 Are all the sections included?
9 Is the document well presented?
10 Are the pages correctly numbered?
11 Is the binding secure?

Summary

Your business plan should be well presented, and free from grammatical and spelling mistakes and typos. The contents should be logical and the writing jargon-free and clear. Any charts or diagrams should be easy to understand. Supporting material should be placed in appendices. Extra non-paper items can be secured in a pouch, zip bag or file. Check everything for completeness and overlooked mistakes before presenting it. Don't forget to back up your plan from the computer regularly and keep a spare paper copy.

11
using the plan

In this chapter you will learn:

- what your plan can do for you
- how to present a business plan
- how to use the plan to run your business
- how to analyse a completed plan

The obvious use for a business plan is to raise money to start the business or enable it to continue or expand. It can also be used as a way to monitor progress and for future planning. In fact, a business plan is something that a business will use continually. It will be changed or replaced over time, but a plan is always necessary for a well-run business.

What can your plan do for you?

In Chapter 1 we described the various reasons for producing a business plan. Here we look at how to use the plan. There are two basic uses for a business plan:

1 raising finance
2 running your business

How to write the financial section of the plan was covered in Chapter 8. Here we discuss presenting the plan to a bank, investors, grant provider or other aid provider. However, raising finance is not the only use for a business plan. Its value as a document for internal use in the business needs to be explained. As we read in Chapter 1, your plan is important as a guide to how to run the business and as such will be constantly referred to.

Presenting your plan

You will already have found out whether a potential lender or investor is willing to consider your plan and whether there is a deadline for reaching them. You will have researched, written, checked, assembled and rechecked your plan as advised in Chapter 10. Now you can post it or hand it in so that it arrives by the deadline.

Always check whether the organization you are approaching with your plan has a specific format for business plans and a specified method of presenting it. Make sure that your plan follows their guidelines in form and content and that you fully understand the procedures for presenting it.

Now you have to wait to see whether you will be asked to take it further by giving a presentation on your plan. What will readers be doing? They will start with the executive summary. Sometimes that is all they will read and your proposal can succeed or fail on that section of the plan alone. If they have time or are interested they might read part or all of the rest of your plan. This initial read of your plan might take anything from a few days to several weeks. You will then be told whether there is enough interest to take it further. If there is, you will probably be asked to meet the readers and present your plan in person and answer any questions they might have.

How the presentation will take place varies. You might simply be asked to discuss your plan further with, for example, your bank manager, or you might be asked to discuss it with several potential lenders or investors. Alternatively, you might be asked to give a full presentation using visual aids.

Whatever the size or type of presentation, you must be prepared to explain your plan in detail and to answer searching questions about any part of it. Expect the questions to be probing and take with you any extra material you need to back up your plan. Read through the plan carefully before the presentation or discussion and try to work out what you might be asked. The financial section is one area that will be discussed in more detail so you need to be sure that you fully understand the financial statements you have included.

Presenting with a partner

You might make the presentation on your own or with one or more partners. Remember, the boss should always lead any presentation of a business plan – if it is your plan, you must present it. However, if you will be sharing a presentation, your partners can help answer questions on their areas of expertise. Agree beforehand which of you will answer questions on which subjects according to your individual strengths.

Be confident

On a personal level the interviewers will expect you to be able to discuss your plan clearly and confidently and to be knowledgeable about it. They will also expect you to show enthusiasm for it. If you do not care, why should they? That does not mean jumping up and down and grinning inanely but looking and talking as if you are genuinely excited about what you are offering in the way of a business opportunity.

Visual aids

If you are expected to give a talk and use visual aids make sure that you prepare them well beforehand. Most computer packages nowadays can help you produce a computer based display (Power Point, for example), or you can use flipcharts and markers or handouts. Whichever you use do not make the sheets too ornate or difficult to read. Keep headings large enough to read from the far side of an average room, and keep lists to no more than three to five points. Keep diagrams clear and uncluttered. It is sensible to use handouts even if you are giving a visual aids presentation. They can be used as a reminder by listeners and will help them follow what you are saying.

If you are not confident about public speaking, practise in front of a mirror. Speak clearly and at normal speed. If you speak too quickly listeners will not catch everything you are saying. Do not just read out what is on the screen or board; explain its importance. Make sure that you also refer to the relevant section in your business plan.

Before you go to the presentation:

1 read through your plan and make a note of potential questions
2 check that you have a copy of your plan, any visual aid materials, handouts and any supplementary information
3 dress neatly (err on the formal side)
4 have a light meal
5 arrive early
6 while waiting, breathe deeply and relax

At the presentation:

1 speak clearly
2 appear confident and enthusiastic
3 ask for questions to be explained, if necessary
4 be honest
5 smile

After the response

You might get a positive response immediately after a presentation or sometime later after the listeners have had time to discuss your project among themselves. If so, you will be told when the business's financial needs will be met and how this will be done, when to fill the forms in and so on. The response might be that amendments are necessary and the plan will need to be considered again. Before making any changes make sure that you find out exactly why they are necessary and what is required. Then make the changes and resubmit. You might, alas, receive the unwelcome news that your plan has failed to impress anyone. Possibly you might be asked to rewrite and resubmit it, but more likely 'no' will mean just that. If so, look at it long and hard before rewriting or resubmitting it elsewhere. Ask yourself these questions:

1 Is my idea good enough? (Check its USP, market, operational capacity.)
2 Is the idea financially sound? (Check and recheck all the financial figures including the potential market and sales.)
3 Is the idea timely? (Has something similar already been done? Has the idea missed a fashion peak?)
4 Can I really put this plan into operation? (Are managers and staff lined up? Are suppliers and distributors organized? Are premises available?)
5 Did I present my idea in the most clear, logical and persuasive way? (Check for basic mistakes, organization of sections, presentation of document, adequate supporting evidence.)
6 Did I approach the right people for help? (Do you need a lender or investor? Are there people who could provide other kinds of help?)
7 Did I fail to impress people at the presentation? (Do you need practice in public speaking? A partner at the presentation? Did you lack enthusiasm?)

Assuming that you have answered all these questions and have rechecked and rewritten the plan in the light of any new research necessary, submit it to someone else. The millionaires of today are the people who never gave up.

Running the business

There are several ways in which your business plan will help you run your business. It can be a guide to where you want to get to as well as a vehicle for communicating within the organization. It will do these things:

- show the way forward
- monitor performance
- assess achievements and weaknesses
- co-ordinate control
- help communication
- empower staff
- generate ideas

The way forward

Once you have finished the plan it comes into its own as a way of monitoring the direction your business will take. You should be constantly comparing what your business is actually doing with how you envisaged it in the plan. There may be times when the business is going in a different direction to the plan, in which case you need to bring it back into line or be able to justify such a change. If business is down and you are not keeping to the plan, you can look at the plan and see where you are going wrong. The plan will change according to the changes you make in the company and it will need to be rewritten every year taking into account necessary changes.

One way of using the plan is to subject it to SWOT analysis. As we have seen in Chapter 3, this is a useful technique for analysing your product or service. However, it can also be used to analyse the plan, and therefore your business, as a whole. Using your business plan as a starting point, analyse it by listing problems and achievements under four headings – Strengths, Weaknesses, Opportunities, Threats.

SWOT your plan

Use the SWOT analysis regularly. It is useful not only as you start to put the plan into action, but also as your business changes and progresses.

Strengths

What are the main things that your business offers? What are you doing well? What techniques and skills are proving particularly beneficial? Have any changes in practices, personnel or ways of working proved particularly successful? Would more similar changes be useful or would new changes be better? In what ways are you doing better than your competitors?

Weaknesses

Be honest here – what could you do better? Are there any areas where customers complain a lot? Is there any obvious area of inefficiency, overspending, understaffing, inadequate skills? Would bringing in outside experts to cast an objective eye over your business practices be helpful? Are your production or service processes out-of-date or inadequate?

Opportunities

Have any of your managers or other employees got under-used or unexploited skills? Would training in new areas open up opportunities? Is there a gap in the market that your product or skill could fill? Is there scope for expansion? Are there marketing opportunities that you haven't taken up yet?

Threats

Are customers moving to your competitors or simply not buying the product or service as much as previously? Are your main competitors the same as when you started the business? Will you come under a financial threat if you overstretch yourself? Are there changes in government regulations or moral and environmental concerns that are affecting your business? Are your staff leaving? Are you getting bad publicity for any reason?

Monitoring performance

Use your plan to monitor performance and manage it. By comparing regularly what you are doing with what you wrote in your plan, you can see where performance needs to be improved or changed. Use the plan to set short- and long-term objectives for individual staff and the business as a whole. We have met the SMART system in this book (see Chapter 2). Use it now to help you monitor the performance of your business as a whole – objectives must be Specific, Measurable, Attainable, Relevant, Time-related.

Specific

Your objectives must be specific, that is do not use vague phrases, such as 'improve performance' but 'increase production by 3 per cent over the next quarter'.

Measurable

How will you know that you've achieved your objectives unless you have a way of measuring them? It might be that you can quantify them (the number of products produced), rely on subjective reports (feedback from customers) or see the results (more advertising on show). However you do it, you need to decide what criteria will constitute success.

Attainable

Trying to overreach yourself will not help you reach objectives. Objectives must be *possible* so becoming a multi-national company may be beyond you, but improving your ranking in your sector of the business market may be possible.

Relevant

You may be able to reduce the number of paperclips your business uses by 10 per cent, but is this a relevant objective? More useful might be to reduce waste by not sending out unnecessary memos.

Time-related

Any objective must be bound by time, that is it must be achievable within a certain time limit. Unless you have a clear idea of when your objectives should be achieved your business will not progress.

Co-ordinate control

Use your plan to ensure that every manager at whatever level in the business knows what should be done and has written guidance about the time each stage should take and who should be doing what. It will also help your managers to understand what time and cost limitations there are so that they can work within them. The plan can be the basis of regular meetings to fine-tune or change the plan so that everyone in the business is working to the same blueprint. Control therefore becomes co-ordinated and effective.

Help communication

By ensuring that everyone in the business sees the plan and understands how it will be put into practice you empower your staff and make them feel part of the business. This motivates them and helps retain staff who feel valued and included. The plan can clarify to everyone what should be happening and leaves less room for mistakes or misunderstandings. An initial meeting to discuss the plan can be beneficial in ensuring your employees' co-operation.

Empower staff

If staff are aware of the expectations for the business you can rely on them more to work in ways that will benefit the company. A clear understanding of the situation and expectations allows you to give more leeway to staff to take their own decisions. With regular reporting back and clear guidance based on the plan, your staff can be empowered to make decisions at their level and thus leave you with more time to concentrate on the overall picture.

Generate ideas

This is an overlooked aspect of using a business plan, but an important one. Once the plan has been written and the business is operating along the lines laid out in the plan it can encourage new ways of thinking from managers and other employees. Staff reading the plan and relating it to their work might think of better ways of doing their jobs, new uses for equipment or innovations in customer service, for example. Ideas can be triggered by reading the plan, which is why it is important that it is used to aid communication amongst staff (see above). Comparing what actually happens to what is written down can create discussion and innovative thinking. The people doing the work are the best people to find new and improved ways of doing things. Encourage responses to the plan, not just when it first comes into use but regularly along the way.

Test
(See page 199 for answers.)
1 What two main areas can you use your plan for?
2 Name two ways the plan can help you run your business.
3 How long should you use your plan for?
4 Who will present your plan?
5 What is the first part of your plan readers will check?

Summary

Your business plan can be used to apply for financial or other aid and to help you run your business. When presenting your plan, be prepared to answer detailed questions about it. If the plan is rejected, check it, reassess it, rewrite it if necessary and present it again to a new potential investor or lender. Use the SWOT and SMART analyses to find out how well your business is performing against the plan. Do not give up!

example business plan

Acme Consulting

January, 1996

This sample business plan has been made available to users of *Business Plan Pro*™, business planning software published by Palo Alto Software. Names, locations and numbers may have been changed, and substantial portions of text may have been omitted to preserve confidentiality and proprietary information. Although this has been revised recently for our 2002 version, we've had to leave the original dates in place because otherwise the discussions of market conditions and industry would seem outdated or unrealistic. This plan was written before the Internet had exploded in 1998–99 and fallen back again in 2000 and 2001.

You are welcome to use this plan as a starting point to create your own, but you do not have permission to reproduce, publish, distribute or even copy this plan as it exists here.

Requests for reprints, academic use, and other dissemination of this sample plan should be addressed to the marketing department of Palo Alto Software. Please e-mail us at info@paloalto.co.uk for more information regarding this sample plan.

Confidentiality Agreement

The undersigned reader acknowledges that the information provided by Acme Consulting in this business plan is confidential; therefore, reader agrees not to disclose it without the express written permission of Acme Consulting.

It is acknowledged by reader that information to be furnished in this business plan is in all respects confidential in nature, other than information which is in the public domain through other means and that any disclosure or use of same by reader, may cause serious harm or damage to Acme Consulting.

Upon request, this document is to be immediately returned to Acme Consulting.

_____

Signature

_____

Name (typed or printed)

_____

Date

This is a business plan. It does not imply an offering of securities.

Table of Contents

1.0 **Executive Summary**

Acme Consulting will be formed as a consulting company specializing in marketing of high-technology products in international markets. Its founders are former marketers of consulting services, personal computers, and market research, all in international markets. They are founding Acme to formalize the consulting services they offer.

Highlights

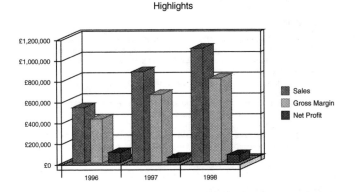

1.1 **Objectives**

1. Sales of £550,000 in 1996 and £1 million by 1998.
2. Gross margin higher than 70%.
3. Net income remains more than 5% of sales through 1998.

1.2 **Mission**

Acme Consulting offers high-tech manufacturers a reliable, high-quality alternative to in-house resources for business development, market development, and channel development on an international scale. A true alternative to in-house resources offers a very high level of practical experience, know-how, contacts, and confidentiality. Clients must know that working with Acme is a more professional, less risky way to develop new areas even than working completely in-house with their own people. Acme must also be able to maintain financial balance, charging a high value for its services, and delivering an even higher value to its clients. Initial focus will be development in the European and Latin American markets, or for European clients in the United Kingdom market.

1.3 Keys to Success

1. Excellence in fulfilling the promise – completely confidential, reliable, trustworthy expertise and information.
2. Developing visibility to generate new business leads.
3. Leveraging from a single pool of expertise into multiple revenue generation opportunities: retainer consulting, project consulting, market research, and market research published reports.

2.0 Company Summary

Acme Consulting is a new company providing high-level expertise in international high-tech business development, channel development, distribution strategies, and marketing of hightech products. It will focus initially on providing two kinds of international triangles:

- Providing United Kingdom clients with development for European and Latin American markets.
- Providing European and United Kingdom clients with development for the United States and Latin American markets.

As it grows it will take on people and consulting work in related markets, such as the rest of Latin America, the Far East, and similar markets. It will also look for additional leverage by taking brokerage positions and representation positions to create percentage holdings in product results.

2.1 Company Ownership

Acme Consulting will be created as a Limited Company based in London, England, owned by its principal investors and principal operators. As of this writing, it has not been registered with Companies House and owners are still considering alternatives of legal formation.

2.2 Start-up Summary

Total start-up expense (including legal costs, logo design, stationery and related expenses) comes to £18,350. Start-up assets required include £32,000 in short-term assets (office furniture, etc.) and £25,000 in initial cash to handle the first few months of consulting operations as sales and accounts receivable play through the cash flow. The details are included in the following table.

Table: Start-up

Start-up	
Requirements	
Start-up Expenses	
Legal	£1,000
Stationery etc.	£3,000
Brochures	£5,000
Consultants	£5,000
Insurance	£350
Expensed equipment	£3,000
Other	£1,000
Total Start-up Expenses	£18,350
Start-up Assets Needed	
Cash Balance on Starting Date	£25,000
Other Current Assets	£7,000
Total Current Assets	£32,000
Long-term Assets	£0
Total Assets	£32,000
Total Requirements	£50,350
Funding	
Investment	
Investor 1	£20,000
Investor 2	£20,000
Other	£10,000
Total Investment	£50,000
Current Liabilities	
Accounts Payable	£350
Current Borrowing	£0
Other Current Liabilities	£0
Current Liabilities	£350
Long-term Liabilities	£0
Total Liabilities	£350
Loss at Start-up	(£18,350)
Total Capital	£31,650
Total Capital and Liabilities	£32,000

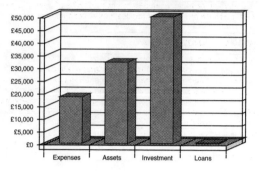

Start-up

2.3 Company Locations and Facilities

The initial office will be established in top quality office space in London's Canary Wharf, as there are high quality office spaces with security and lobby areas. It is important for a high tech consulting company to spend money on high quality centrally located office space.

3.0 Services

Acme offers the expertise a high-technology company needs to develop new product distribution and new market segments in new markets. This can be taken as high-level retainer consulting, market research reports, or project-based consulting.

3.1 Service Description

1. **Retainer consulting:** We represent a client company as an extension of its business development and market development functions. This begins with complete understanding of the client company's situation, objectives, and constraints. We then represent the client company quietly and confidentially, sifting through new market developments and new opportunities as is appropriate to the client, representing the client in initial talks with possible allies, vendors, and channels.

2. **Project consulting:** Proposed and billed on a per-project and per-milestone basis, project consulting offers a client company a way to harness our specific qualities and use our expertise to solve specific problems, develop and/or implement plans, and develop specific information.

3. **Market research:** Group studies available to selected clients at £5,000 per unit. A group study is a packaged and published complete study of a specific market, channel, or topic. Examples might be studies of developing consumer channels in France or Mexico, or implications of changing margins in software.

3.2 Competitive Comparison

The competition comes in several forms:

1. The most significant competition is no consulting at all, companies choosing to do business development, channel development and market research in-house. Their own managers do this on their own, as part of their regular business functions. Our key advantage in competition with in-house development is that managers are already overloaded with responsibilities, they don't have time for additional responsibilities in new market development or new channel development. Also, Acme can approach alliances, vendors, and channels on a confidential basis, gathering information and making initial contacts in ways that the corporate managers can't.

2. The high-level prestige management consulting: McKinsey, Bain, Accenture, etc. These are essentially generalists who take their name-brand management consulting into specialty areas. Most of these are US firms that have expanded to the UK and have offices in London and all over continental Europe. Their other very important weakness is the management structure that has the partners selling new jobs, and inexperienced associates delivering the work. We compete against them as experts in our specific fields, and with the guarantee that our clients will have the top-level people doing the actual work.

3. The third general kind of competitor is the international market research company: International Data Corporation (IDC), Dataquest, etc. These companies are formidable competitors for published market research and market forums, but cannot provide the kind of high-level consulting that Acme will provide.

4. The fourth kind of competition is the market-specific smaller house. For example: Gloucestershire Research in the United Kingdom, Select S.A. de C.V. in Mexico (now affiliated with IDC).

5. Sales representation, brokering, and deal catalysts are an ad-hoc business form that will be defined in detail by the specific nature of each individual case.

3.3 Sales Literature

The business will begin with a general corporate brochure establishing the positioning. This brochure will be developed as part of the start-up expenses. Literature and mailings for the initial market forums will be very important.

3.4 Fulfilment

1. The key fulfilment and delivery will be provided by the principals of the business. The real core value is professional expertise, provided by a combination of experience, hard work, and education (in that order).

2. We will turn to qualified professionals for freelance back-up in market research and presentation and report development, which are areas that we can afford to subcontract without risking the core values provided to the clients.

3.5 Technology

Acme Consulting will maintain the latest Windows and Macintosh capabilities including:

1. Complete e-mail facilities on the Internet, CompuServe, America Online, and Applelink, for working with clients directly through e-mail delivery of drafts and information.

2. Complete presentation facilities for preparation and delivery of multimedia presentations on Macintosh or Windows machines, in formats including on-disk presentation, live presentation, or video presentation.

3. Complete desktop publishing facilities for delivery of regular retainer reports, project output reports, marketing materials, and market research reports.

3.6 Future Services

In the future, Acme will broaden the coverage by expanding into coverage of additional markets (e.g., all of Latin America, Far East,) and additional product areas (e.g., telecommunications and technology integration).
We are also studying the possibility of newsletter or electronic newsletter services, or perhaps special on-topic reports.

4.0 Market Analysis Summary

Acme will be focusing on high-technology manufacturers of computer hardware and software, services, and networking, who want to sell into markets in the United States, Europe, and Latin America. These are mostly larger companies, and occasionally medium-sized companies. Our most important group of potential customers are executives in larger corporations. These are marketing managers, general managers, sales managers, sometimes charged with international focus and sometimes charged with market or even specific channel focus. They do not want to waste their time or risk their money looking for bargain information or questionable expertise. As they go into markets looking at new opportunities, they are very sensitive to risking their company's name and reputation.

4.1 Market Segmentation

Large manufacturer corporations: Our most important market segment is the large manufacturer corporations of high-technology products, such as Apple, Hewlett-Packard, IBM, Microsoft, Siemens, or Olivetti. These companies will be calling on Acme for development functions that are better spun off than managed in-house, for market research, and for market forums. Medium-sized growth companies: Particularly in software, multimedia, and some related highgrowth fields, Acme will offer an attractive development alternative to the company that is management constrained and unable to address opportunities in new markets and new market segments.

Market Analysis (Pie)

- ■ U.S. High Tech
- ▧ European High Tech
- ■ Latin America
- ░ Other

Table: Market Analysis

Market Analysis Potential Customers	Growth	1996	1997	1998	1999	2000	CAGR
U.S. High Tech	10%	5,000	5,500	6,050	6,655	7,321	10.00%
European High Tech	15%	1,000	1,150	1,323	1,521	1,749	15.00%
Latin America	35%	250	338	456	616	832	35.07%
Other	2%	10,000	10,200	10,404	10,612	10,824	2.00%
Total	6.27%	16,250	17,188	18,233	19,404	20,726	6.27%

4.2 Target Market Segment Strategy

As indicated by the previous table and Illustration, we must focus on a few thousand well-chosen potential customers in Europe and Latin America, while also offering services to US firms that want to expand into European markets. These few thousand high-tech manufacturing companies are the key customers for Acme.

4.3 Service Business Analysis

The consulting "industry" is pulverized and disorganized, with thousands of smaller consulting organizations and individual consultants for every one of the few dozen well-known companies.

Consulting participants range from major international name-brand consultants to tens of thousands of individuals. One of Acme's challenges will be establishing itself as a *real* consulting company, positioned as a relatively risk-free corporate purchase.

4.3.1 Business Participants

At the highest level are the few well-established major names in management consulting. Most of these are organized as partnerships established in major markets around the world, linked together by interconnecting directors and sharing the name and corporate wisdom. Some evolved from accounting companies (e.g. Arthur Andersen, Touche Ross) and some from management consulting (McKinsey, Bain). These companies charge very high rates for consulting, and maintain relatively high overhead structures and fulfilment structures based on partners selling and junior associates fulfiling.

At the intermediate level are some function-specific or market-specific consultants, such as the market research firms (IDC, Dataquest) or channel development firms (ChannelCorp, Channel Strategies, ChannelMark).

Some kinds of consulting are little more than contract expertise provided by somebody who, while temporarily out of work, offers consulting services.

4.3.2 Distribution Patterns

Consulting is sold and purchased mainly on a word-of-mouth basis, with relationships and previous experience being, by far, the most important factor. The major name-brand houses have locations in major cities and major markets, and executive-level managers or partners develop new business through industry associations, business associations, chambers of commerce and industry, etc., and in some cases social associations such as country clubs.

The medium-level houses are generally area specific or function specific, and are not easily able to leverage their business through distribution.

4.3.3 Competition and Buying Patterns

The key element in purchase decisions made at the Acme client level is trust in the professional reputation and reliability of the consulting firm.

4.3.4 Main Competitors

1. The high-level prestige management consulting firms:

Strengths: International locations managed by owner-partners with a high level of presentation and understanding of general business. Enviable reputations which make purchase of consulting an easy decision for a manager, despite the very high prices.

Weaknesses: General business knowledge doesn't substitute for the specific market, channel, and distribution expertise of Acme, focusing on high-technology markets and products only. Also, fees are extremely expensive, and work is generally done by very junior-level consultants, even though sold by high-level partners.

2. The international market research company:

Strengths: International offices, specific market knowledge, permanent staff developing market research information on permanent basis, good relationships with potential client companies.

Weaknesses: Market numbers are not marketing, not channel development nor market development. Although these companies compete for some of the business Acme is after, they cannot really offer the same level of business understanding at a high level.

3. Market specific or function specific experts:

Strengths: Expertise in market or functional areas. Acme should not try to compete with Gloucestershire Research or Accenture, or Select in their markets with market research, or with ChannelCorp in channel management.

Weaknesses: The inability to spread beyond a specific focus, or to rise above a specific focus, to provide actual management expertise, experience, and wisdom beyond the specifics.

4. Companies do in-house research and development:

Strengths: No incremental cost except travel; also, the general work is done by the people who are entirely responsible, the planning is done by those who will implement it.

Weaknesses: Most managers are terribly overburdened already, unable to find incremental resources in time and people to apply to incremental opportunities. Also, there is a lot of additional risk in market and channel development done in-house from the ground up. Finally, retainer-based antenna consultants can greatly enhance a company's reach and extend its position into conversations that might otherwise never have taken place.

5.0 **Strategy and Implementation Summary**

Acme will focus on three geographical markets, Europe, Latin America, and the United States, and in limited product segments: personal computers, software, networks, telecommunication, personal organizers, and technology integration products.

The target customer is usually a manager in a larger corporation, and occasionally an owner or president of a medium-sized corporation in a high-growth period.

5.1 **Untitled**

Acme Consulting will be priced at the upper edge of what the market will bear, competing with the name-brand consultants. The pricing fits with the general positioning of Acme as providing high-level expertise.
Consulting should be based on £3,000 per day for project consulting, £1,500 per day for market research, and £7,000 per month and up for retainer consulting. Market research reports should be priced at £3,000 per report, which will, of course, require that reports be very well planned, focused on very important topics, and very well presented.

5.2 **Sales Strategy**

The sales forecast monthly summary is included in the appendix. The annual sales projections are included here in the table on the following page.

Sales by Year

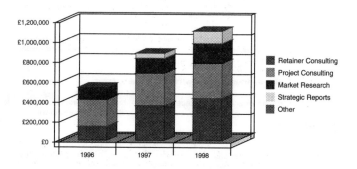

Table: Sales Forecast

Sales Forecast			
Sales	1996	1997	1998
Retainer Consulting	£140,000	£350,000	£425,000
Project Consulting	£270,000	£325,000	£350,000
Market Research	£122,000	£150,000	£200,000
Strategic Reports	£0	£50,000	£125,000
Other	£0	£0	£0
Total Sales	£532,000	£875,000	£1,100,000
Direct Cost of Sales	1996	1997	1998
Retainer Consulting	£21,200	£38,000	£48,000
Project Consulting	£29,550	£56,000	£70,000
Market Research	£57,250	£105,000	£131,000
Strategic Reports	£0	£20,000	£40,000
Other	£0	£0	£0
Subtotal Direct Cost of Sales	£108,000	£219,000	£289,000

Sales Monthly

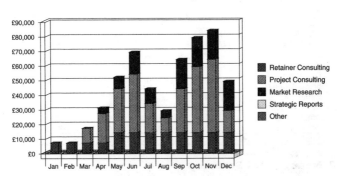

5.3 Milestones

Our detailed milestones are shown in the following table and chart. The related budgets are included with the expenses shown in the projected Profit and Loss statement, which is in the financial analysis that comes in Chapter 7 of this plan.

Acme Consulting

Milestones

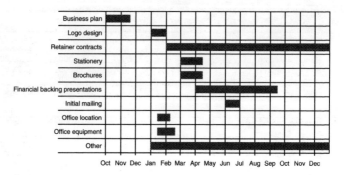

Oct Nov Dec Jan Feb Mar Apr May Jun Jul Aug Sep Oct Nov Dec

Table: Milestones

| Milestones | | | | | |
Milestone	Start Date	End Date	Budget	Manager	Department
Business plan	10/1/1995	11/19/1995	£3,500	HM	Devpt
Logo design	1/1/1996	2/1/1996	£1,500	TAJ	Marketing
Retainer contracts	2/1/1996	12/31 /1996	£7,000	HM	Sales
Stationery	3/1/1996	4/15/1996	£300	JD	G&A
Brochures	3/1/1996	4/15/1996	£1,700	TAJ	Marketing
Financial backing presentations	4/1/1996	9/15/1996	£7,000	HM	Devpt
Initial mailing	6/1/1996	7/1/1996	£3,000	HM	Sales
Office location	1/15/1996	2/9/1996	£3,000	JD	G&A
Office equipment	1/15/1996	2/19/1996	£8,000	JD	G&A
Other	1/1/1996	12/31/1996	£7,000	ABC	Department
Totals			£42,000		

6.0 Management Summary

The initial management team depends on the founders themselves, with little back-up. As we grow, we will take on additional consulting help, plus graphic/editorial, sales, and marketing.

6.1 Organizational Structure

Acme should be managed by working partners, in a structure taken mainly from Smith Partners. In the beginning we assume 3–5 partners:
- Ralph Sampson.
- At least one, probably two, partners from Smith and Jones.
- One strong United States partner, based in San Francisco.
- The organization has to be very flat in the beginning, with each of the founders responsible for his or her own work and management.
- One other strong partner.

6.2 Management Team

The Acme business requires a very high level of international experience and expertise, which means that it will not be easily leveragable in the common consulting company mode in which partners run the business and make sales, while associates fulfil. Partners will necessarily be involved in the fulfilment of the core business proposition, providing the expertise to the clients. The initial personnel plan is still tentative. It should involve 3–5 partners, 1–3 consultants, one strong editorial/graphic person with good staff support, one strong marketing person, an office manager, and a secretary. Later, we add more partners, consultants, and sales staff. Founders' resumes are included as an attachment to this plan.

6.3 Personnel Plan

The detailed monthly personnel plan for the first year is included in the appendix. The annual personnel estimates are included here.

Table: Personnel

Personnel Plan			
	1996	1997	1998
Partners	£96,000	£175,000	£200,000
Consultants	£0	£50,000	£63,000
Editorial/graphic	£12,000	£14,000	£17,000
VP Marketing	£14,000	£50,000	£55,000
Sales people	£0	£30,000	£33,000
Office Manager	£5,250	£30,000	£33,000
Secretarial	£5,250	£20,000	£22,000
Other	£0	£0	£0
Other	£0	£0	£0
Total People	7	14	20
Total Payroll	£132,500	£369,000	£423,000

7.0 Financial Plan

Our financial plan is based on conservative estimates and assumptions. We will need to plan on initial investment to make the financials work.

7.1 Important Assumptions

Table 7.1 summarizes key financial assumptions, including sales entirely on invoice basis, payroll burden, and present-day interest and taxation rates.

We also assume 45-day average collection days, expenses mainly on net 30 basis and 35 days on average for payment of invoices.

Table: General Assumptions

General Assumptions			
	1996	1997	1998
Plan Month	1	2	3
Current Interest Rate	8.00%	8.00%	8.00%
Long-term Interest Rate	10.00%	10.00%	10.00%
Tax Rate	25.00%	25.00%	25.00%
Sales on Credit %	100.00%	100.00%	100.00%
Other	0	0	0

7.2 Key Financial Indicators

The following benchmark chart indicates our key financial indicators for the first three years. We foresee major growth in sales and operating expenses, and a bump in our collection days as we spread the business during expansion.

Benchmarks

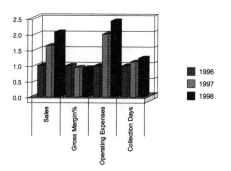

7.3 Break-even Analysis

Table 7.3 summarizes the break-even analysis, including monthly units and sales break-even points.

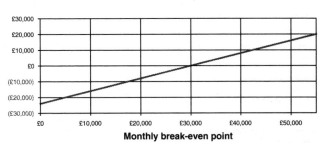

Break-even Analysis

Monthly break-even point

Break-even point = where line intersects with 0

Table: Break-even Analysis

Break-even Analysis:	
Monthly Units Break-even	29,985
Monthly Revenue Break-even	£29,985

Assumptions:	
Average Per-Unit Revenue	£1.00
Average Per-Unit Variable Cost	£0.20
Estimated Monthly Fixed Cost	£23,988

Acme Consulting

7.4 Projected Profit and Loss

The detailed monthly pro-forma income statement for the first year is included in the appendix. The annual estimates are included here.

Table: Profit and Loss

Pro Forma Profit and Loss			
	1996	1997	1998
Sales	£532,000	£875,000	£1,100,000
Direct Cost of Sales	£108,000	£219,000	£289,000
Other	£0	£0	£0
Total Cost of Sales	£108,000	£219,000	£289,000
Gross Margin	£424,000	£656,000	£811,000
Gross Margin %	79.70%	74.97%	73.73%
Expenses:			
Payroll	£132,500	£369,000	£423,000
Sales and Marketing and Other Expenses	£108,600	£137,000	£195,000
Depreciation	£0	£0	£0
Leased Equipment	£3,600	£7,000	£7,000
Utilities	£9,000	£12,000	£12,000
Insurance	£3,600	£2,000	£2,000
Rent	£12,000	£0	£0
Other	£0	£0	£0
Payroll Taxes	£18,550	£51,660	£59,220
Other	£0	£0	£0
Total Operating Expenses	£287,850	£578,660	£698,220
Profit Before Interest and Taxes	£136,150	£77,340	£112,780
Interest Expense	£6,800	£11,400	£15,400
Taxes Incurred	£32,338	£16,485	£24,345
Net Profit	£97,013	£49,455	£73,035
Net Profit/Sales	18.24%	5.65%	6.64%

7.5 Projected Cash Flow

Cash flow projections are critical to our success. The monthly cash flow is shown in the illustration, with one bar representing the cash flow per month and the other representing the monthly balance. The annual cash flow figures are included here as shown on the table on the following page. Detailed monthly numbers are included in the appendix.

Cash

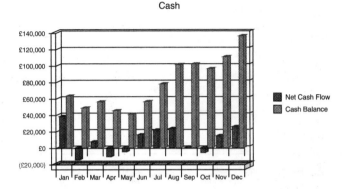

Acme Consulting

Table: Cash Flow

Pro Forma Cash Flow			
	1996	1997	1998
Cash Received			
Cash from Operations:			
Cash Sales	£0	£0	£0
Cash from Receivables	£443,800	£818,134	£1,062,697
Subtotal Cash from Operations	£443,800	£818,134	£1,062,697
Additional Cash Received			
Sales Tax, VAT, HST/GST Received	£77,665	£0	£0
New Current Borrowing	£30,000	£100,000	£0
New Other Liabilities (interest-free)	£0	£0	£0
New Long-term Liabilities	£50,000	£0	£0
Sales of Other Current Assets	£0	£0	£0
Sales of Long-term Assets	£0	£0	£0
New Investment Received	£0	£0	£0
Subtotal Cash Received	£601,465	£918,134	£1,062,697
Expenditures	1996	1997	1998
Expenditures from Operations:			
Cash Spending	£70,984	£101,221	£136,186
Payment of Accounts Payable	£341,443	£714,565	£879,494
Subtotal Spent on Operations	£412,427	£815,786	£1,015,680
Additional Cash Spent			
Sales Tax, VAT, HST/GST Paid Out	£77,665	£0	£0
Principal Repayment of Current Borrowing	£0	£0	£0
Other Liabilities Principal Repayment	£0	£0	£0
Long-term Liabilities Principal Repayment	£0	£0	£0
Purchase Other Current Assets	£0	£0	£0
Purchase Long-term Assets	£0	£0	£0
Dividends	£0	£0	£0
Subtotal Cash Spent	£490,092	£815,786	£1,015,680
Net Cash Flow	£111,373	£102,348	£47,017
Cash Balance	£136,373	£238,721	£285,739

7.6 Projected Balance Sheet

The balance sheet shows healthy growth of net worth, and strong financial position.
The monthly estimates are included in the appendix.

Table: Balance Sheet

Pro Forma Balance Sheet

Assets

Current Assets	1996	1997	1998
Cash	£136,373	£238,721	£285,739
Accounts Receivable	£88,200	£145,066	£182,368
Other Current Assets	£7,000	£7,000	£7,000
Total Current Assets	£231,573	£390,787	£475,107
Long-term Assets			
Long-term Assets	£0	£0	£0
Accumulated Depreciation	£0	£0	£0
Total Long-term Assets	£0	£0	£0
Total Assets	£231,573	£390,787	£475,107

Liabilities and Capital			
Current Liabilities	1996	1997	1998
Accounts Payable	£22,910	£32,669	£43,954
Current Borrowing	£30,000	£130,000	£130,000
Other Current Liabilities	£0	£0	£0
Subtotal Current Liabilities	£52,910	£162,669	£173,954
Long-term Liabilities	£50,000	£50,000	£50,000
Total Liabilities	£102,910	£212,669	£223,954
Paid-in Capital	£50,000	£50,000	£50,000
Retained Earnings	(£18,350)	£78,663	£128,118
Earnings	£97,013	£49,455	£73,035
Total Capital	£128,663	£178,118	£251,153
Total Liabilities and Capital	£231,573	£390,787	£475,107
Net Worth	£128,663	£178,118	£251,153

7.7 Business Ratios

The following table shows the projected business ratios. We expect to maintain
healthy ratios for profitability, risk, and return. The industry comparisons are for
U.S. Standard Industrial Classification (SIC) Index code 8742, Management
Consulting Services.

Acme Consulting

Table: Ratios

Ratio Analysis				Industry
	1996	1997	1998	Profile
Sales Growth	0.00%	64.47%	25.71 %	8.60%
Percent of Total Assets				
Accounts Receivable	38.09%	37.12%	38.38%	24.40%
Inventory	0.00%	0.00%	0.00%	3.80%
Other Current Assets	3.02%	1.79%	1.47%	46.70%
Total Current Assets	100.00%	100.00%	100.00%	74.90%
Long-term Assets	0.00%	0.00%	0.00%	25.10%
Total Assets	100.00%	100.00%	100.00%	100.00%
Current Liabilities	22.85%	41.63%	36.61 %	42.80%
Long-term Liabilities	21.59%	12.79%	10.52%	17.20%
Total Liabilities	44.44%	54.42%	47.14%	60.00%
Net Worth	55.56%	45.58%	52.86%	40.00%
Percent of Sales				
Sales	100.00%	100.00%	100.00%	100.00%
Gross Margin	79.70%	74.97%	73.73%	100.00%
Selling, General and Administrative Expenses	61.46%	69.32%	67.09%	83.50%
Advertising Expenses	4.51%	4.57%	4.00%	1.20%
Profit Before Interest and Taxes	25.59%	8.84%	10.25%	2.60%
Main Ratios				
Current	4.38	2.40	2.73	1.59
Quick	4.38	2.40	2.73	1.26
Total Debt to Total Assets	44.44%	54.42%	47.14%	60.00%
Pre-tax Return on Net Worth	100.53%	37.02%	38.77%	4.40%
Pre-tax Return on Assets	55.86%	16.87%	20.50%	10.90%
Additional Ratios	1996	1997	1998	
Net Profit Margin	18.24%	5.65%	6.64%	n.a
Return on Equity	75.40%	27.77%	29.08%	n.a
Activity Ratios				
Accounts Receivable Turnover	6.03	6.03	6.03	n.a
Collection Days	43	49	54	n.a
Inventory Turnover	0.00	0.00	0.00	n.a
Accounts Payable Turnover	15.89	22.17	20.27	n.a
Payment Days	18	14	16	n.a
Total Asset Turnover	2.30	2.24	2.32	n.a
Debt Ratios				
Debt to Net Worth	0.80	1.19	0.89	n.a
Current Liab. to Liab.	0.51	0.76	0.78	n.a
Liquidity Ratios				
Net Working Capital	£178,663	£228,118	£301,153	n.a
Interest Coverage	20.02	6.78	7.32	n.a
Additional Ratios				
Assets to Sales	0.44	0.45	0.43	n.a
Current Debt/Total Assets	23%	42%	37%	n.a
Acid Test	2.71	1.51	1.68	n.a
Sales/Net Worth	4.13	4.91	4.38	n.a
Dividend Payout	0.00	0.00	0.00	n.a

Appendix

Appendix Table: Sales Forecast

Sales Forecast

Sales	Jan	Feb	Mar	Apr	May	Jun	Jul	Aug	Sep	Oct	Nov	Dec
Retainer Consulting	£7,000	£7,000	£7,000	£7,000	£14,000	£14,000	£14,000	£14,000	£14,000	£14,000	£14,000	£14,000
Project Consulting	£0	£0	£10,000	£20,000	£30,000	£40,000	£20,000	£10,000	£30,000	£45,000	£50,000	£15,000
Market Research	£0	£0	£0	£4,000	£8,000	£15,000	£10,000	£5,000	£20,000	£20,000	£20,000	£20,000
Strategic Reports	£0	£0	£0	£0	£0	£0	£0	£0	£0	£0	£0	£0
Other	£0	£0	£0	£0	£0	£0	£0	£0	£0	£0	£0	£0
Total Sales	£7,000	£7,000	£17,000	£31,000	£52,000	£69,000	£44,000	£29,000	£64,000	£79,000	£84,000	£49,000

Direct Cost of Sales	Jan	Feb	Mar	Apr	May	Jun	Jul	Aug	Sep	Oct	Nov	Dec
Retainer Consulting	£2,500	£1,700	£1,700	£1,700	£1,700	£1,700	£1,700	£1,700	£1,700	£1,700	£1,700	£1,700
Project Consulting	£0	£0	£700	£2,700	£3,000	£4,250	£2,250	£700	£3,000	£5,000	£6,250	£1,700
Market Research	£0	£0	£0	£1,500	£4,000	£7,000	£4,000	£2,750	£9,500	£9,500	£9,500	£9,500
Strategic Reports	£0	£0	£0	£0	£0	£0	£0	£0	£0	£0	£0	£0
Other	£0	£0	£0	£0	£0	£0	£0	£0	£0	£0	£0	£0
Subtotal Direct Cost of Sales	£2,500	£1,700	£2,400	£5,900	£8,700	£12,950	£7,950	£5,150	£14,200	£16,200	£17,450	£12,900

Appendix

Appendix Table: Personnel

Personnel Plan

		Jan	Feb	Mar	Apr	May	Jun	Jul	Aug	Sep	Oct	Nov	Dec
Partners	140%	£8,000	£8,000	£8,000	£8,000	£8,000	£8,000	£8,000	£8,000	£8,000	£8,000	£8,000	£8,000
Consultants	125%	£0	£0	£0	£0	£0	£0	£0	£0	£0	£4,000	£4,000	£4,000
Editorial/graphic	120%	£0	£0	£0	£0	£0	£0	£0	£0	£3,500	£3,500	£3,500	£3,500
VP Marketing	110%	£0	£0	£0	£0	£0	£0	£0	£0	£0	£0	£0	£0
Sales people	110%	£0	£0	£0	£0	£0	£0	£0	£0	£0	£0	£0	£0
Office Manager	110%	£0	£0	£0	£0	£0	£0	£0	£0	£0	£ 1,750	£1,750	£1,750
Secretarial	110%	£0	£0	£0	£0	£0	£0	£0	£0	£0	£ 1,750	£1,750	£1,750
Other	110%	£0	£0	£0	£0	£0	£0	£0	£0	£0	£0	£0	£0
Other		£0	£0	£0	£0	£0	£0	£0	£0	£0	£0	£0	£0
Total People		3	3	3	3	3	3	3	3	5	7	7	7
Total Payroll		£8,000	£8,000	£8,000	£8,000	£8,000	£8,000	£8,000	£8,000	£11,500	£19,000	£19,000	£19,000

Acme Consulting; © [2001] Palo Alto Software, Inc.
(www.paloalto.com) reproduced with permission.
Created in Business Plan Pro®

Appendix

Appendix Table: General Assumptions

General Assumptions	Jan	Feb	Mar	Apr	May	Jun	Jul	Aug	Sep	Oct	Nov	Dec
Plan Month	1	2	3	4	5	6	7	8	9	10	11	12
Current Interest Rate	8.00%	8.00%	8.00%	8.00%	8.00%	8.00%	8.00%	8.00%	8.00%	8.00%	8.00%	8.00%
Long-term Interest Rate	10.00%	10.00%	10.00%	10.00%	10.00%	10.00%	10.00%	10.00%	10.00%	10.00%	10.00%	10.00%
Tax Rate	25.00%	25.00%	25.00%	25.00%	25.00%	25.00%	25.00%	25.00%	25.00%	25.00%	25.00%	25.00%
Sales on Credit %	100.00%	100.00%	100.00%	100.00%	100.00%	100.00%	100.00%	100.00%	100.00%	100.00%	100.00%	100.00%
Other	0	0	0	0	0	0	0	0	0	0	0	0

Appendix

Appendix Table: Profit and Loss

Pro Forma Profit and Loss

	Jan	Feb	Mar	Apr	May	Jun	Jul	Aug	Sep	Oct	Nov	Dec
Sales	£7,000	£7,000	£17,000	£31,000	£52,000	£69,000	£44,000	£29,000	£64,000	£79,000	£84,000	£49,000
Direct Cost of Sales	£2,500	£1,700	£2,400	£5,900	£8,700	£12,950	£7,950	£5,150	£14,200	£16,200	£17,450	£12,900
Other	£0	£0	£0	£0	£0	£0	£0	£0	£0	£0	£0	£0
Total Cost of Sales	£2,500	£1,700	£2,400	£5,900	£8,700	£12,950	£7,950	£5,150	£14,200	£16,200	£17,450	£12,900
Gross Margin	£4,500	£5,300	£14,600	£25,100	£43,300	£56,050	£36,050	£23,850	£49,800	£62,800	£66,550	£36,100
Gross Margin %	64.29%	75.71%	85.88%	80.97%	83.27%	81.23%	81.93%	82.24%	77.81%	79.49%	79.23%	73.67%
Expenses:												
Payroll	£8,000	£8,000	£8,000	£8,000	£8,000	£8,000	£8,000	£8,000	£11,500	£19,000	£19,000	£19,000
Sales and Marketing and Other Expenses	£9,050	£9,050	£9,050	£9,050	£9,050	£9,050	£9,050	£9,050	£9,050	£9,050	£9,050	£9,050
Depreciation	£0	£0	£0	£0	£0	£0	£0	£0	£0	£0	£0	£0
Leased Equipment	£300	£300	£300	£300	£300	£300	£300	£300	£300	£300	£300	£300
Utilities	£750	£750	£750	£750	£750	£750	£750	£750	£750	£750	£750	£750
Insurance	£300	£300	£300	£300	£300	£300	£300	£300	£300	£300	£300	£300
Rent	£1,000	£1,000	£1,000	£1,000	£1,000	£1,000	£1,000	£1,000	£1,000	£1,000	£1,000	£1,000
Other	£0	£0	£0	£0	£0	£0	£0	£0	£0	£0	£0	£0
Payroll Taxes 14%	£1,120	£1,120	£1,120	£1,120	£1,120	£1,120	£1,120	£1,120	£1,610	£2,660	£2,660	£2,660
Other	£0	£0	£0	£0	£0	£0	£0	£0	£0	£0	£0	£0
Total Operating Expenses	£20,520	£20,520	£20,520	£20,520	£20,520	£20,520	£20,520	£20,520	£24,510	£33,060	£33,060	£33,060
Profit Before Interest and Taxes	(£16,020)	(£15,220)	(£5,920)	£4,580	£22,780	£35,530	£15,530	£3,330	£25,290	£29,740	£33,490	£33,060
Interest Expense	£417	£417	£550	£550	£617	£617	£617	£617	£617	£617	£617	£617
Taxes Incurred	(£4,109)	(£3,909)	(£1,618)	£1,008	£5,558	£8,728	£3,728	£678	£6,168	£7,281	£8,218	£606
Net Profit	(£12,328)	(£11,728)	(£4,853)	£3,023	£16,673	£26,185	£11,185	£2,035	£18,505	£21,843	£24,655	£1,818
Net Profit/Sales	-176.11%	-167.54%	-28.54%	9.75%	32.06%	37.95%	25.42%	7.02%	28.91%	27.65%	29.35%	3.71%

Appendix

Appendix Table: Cash Flow

Pro Forma Cash Flow		Jan	Feb	Mar	Apr	May	Jun	Jul	Aug	Sep	Oct	Nov	Dec
Cash Received													
Cash from Operations:													
Cash Sales		£0	£3,733	£7,000	£12,333	£24,467	£42,200	£61,067	£55,667	£36,000	£47,667	£72,000	£81,667
Cash from Receivables		£0	£0	£0	£0	£0	£0	£0	£0	£0	£0	£0	£0
Subtotal Cash from Operations		£0	£3,733	£7,000	£12,333	£24,467	£42,200	£61,067	£55,667	£36,000	£47,667	£72,000	£81,667
Additional Cash Received													
Sales Tax, VAT, HST/GST Received	17.50%	£0	£653	£1,225	£2,158	£4,282	£7,385	£10,687	£9,742	£6,300	£8,342	£12,600	£14,292
New Current Borrowing		£0	£0	£20,000	£0	£0	£10,000	£0	£0	£0	£0	£0	£0
New Other Liabilities (interest-free)		£0	£0	£0	£0	£0	£0	£0	£0	£0	£0	£0	£0
New Long-term Liabilities		£50,000	£0	£0	£0	£0	£0	£0	£0	£0	£0	£0	£0
Sales of Other Current Assets		£0	£0	£0	£0	£0	£0	£0	£0	£0	£0	£0	£0
Sales of Long-term Assets		£0	£0	£0	£0	£0	£0	£0	£0	£0	£0	£0	£0
New Investment Received		£0	£0	£0	£0	£0	£0	£0	£0	£0	£0	£0	£0
Subtotal Cash Received		£50,000	£4,387	£28,225	£14,492	£28,748	£59,585	£71,735	£65,408	£42,300	£56,008	£84,600	£95,958
Expenditures													
Expenditures from Operations:													
Cash Spending		£2,552	£2,402	£3,183	£4,714	£6,552	£8,424	£5,924	£4,461	£8,096	£8,874	£9,421	£6,381
Payment of Accounts Payable		£9,420	£15,798	£16,393	£18,357	£22,651	£28,041	£33,643	£27,891	£27,079	£44,495	£47,972	£49,705
Subtotal Spent on Operations		£11,972	£18,200	£19,576	£23,071	£29,203	£36,464	£39,566	£32,353	£35,175	£53,369	£57,393	£56,086
Additional Cash Spent													
Sales Tax, VAT, HST/GST Paid Out		£0	£653	£1,225	£2,158	£4,282	£7,385	£10,687	£9,742	£6,300	£8,342	£12,600	£14,292
Principal Repayment of Current Borrowing		£0	£0	£0	£0	£0	£0	£0	£0	£0	£0	£0	£0
Other Liabilities Principal Repayment		£0	£0	£0	£0	£0	£0	£0	£0	£0	£0	£0	£0
Long-term Liabilities Principal Repayment		£0	£0	£0	£0	£0	£0	£0	£0	£0	£0	£0	£0
Purchase Other Current Assets		£0	£0	£0	£0	£0	£0	£0	£0	£0	£0	£0	£0
Purchase Long-term Assets		£0	£0	£0	£0	£0	£0	£0	£0	£0	£0	£0	£0
Dividends		£0	£0	£0	£0	£0	£0	£0	£0	£0	£0	£0	£0
Subtotal Cash Spent		£11,972	£18,853	£20,801	£25,230	£33,484	£43,849	£50,253	£42,094	£41,475	£61,711	£69,993	£70,377
Net Cash Flow		£38,028	(£14,466)	£7,424	(£10,738)	(£4,736)	£15,736	£21,500	£23,314	£825	(£5,702)	£14,607	£25,581
Cash Balance		£63,028	£48,562	£55,986	£45,248	£40,512	£56,248	£77,748	£101,062	£101,887	£96,185	£110,792	£136,373

Appendix

Appendix Table: Balance Sheet

Pro Forma Balance Sheet

	Starting Balances	Jan	Feb	Mar	Apr	May	Jun	Jul	Aug	Sep	Oct	Nov	Dec
Assets													
Current Assets													
Cash	£25,000	£63,028	£48,562	£55,986	£45,248	£40,512	£56,248	£77,748	£101,062	£101,887	£96,185	£110,792	£136,373
Accounts Receivable	£0	£7,000	£10,267	£20,267	£38,933	£66,467	£93,267	£76,200	£49,533	£77,533	£108,867	£120,867	£88,200
Other Current Assets	£7,000	£7,000	£7,000	£7,000	£7,000	£7,000	£7,000	£7,000	£7,000	£7,000	£7,000	£7,000	£7,000
Total Current Assets	£32,000	£77,028	£65,829	£83,253	£91,181	£113,979	£156,515	£160,948	£157,596	£186,421	£212,052	£238,659	£231,573
Long-term Assets													
Long-term Assets	£0	£0	£0	£0	£0	£0	£0	£0	£0	£0	£0	£0	£0
Accumulated Depreciation	£0	£0	£0	£0	£0	£0	£0	£0	£0	£0	£0	£0	£0
Total Long-term Assets	£0	£0	£0	£0	£0	£0	£0	£0	£0	£0	£0	£0	£0
Total Assets	£32,000	£77,028	£65,829	£83,253	£91,181	£113,979	£156,515	£160,948	£157,596	£186,421	£212,052	£238,659	£231,573
Liabilities and Capital													
Current Liabilities													
Accounts Payable	£350	£7,706	£8,234	£10,510	£15,416	£21,541	£27,892	£21,141	£15,753	£26,073	£29,862	£31,814	£22,910
Current Borrowing	£0	£0	£0	£0	£20,000	£20,000	£30,000	£30,000	£30,000	£30,000	£30,000	£30,000	£30,000
Other Current Liabilities	£0	£0	£0	£0	£0	£0	£0	£0	£0	£0	£0	£0	£0
Subtotal Current Liabilities	£350	£7,706	£8,234	£30,510	£35,416	£41,541	£57,892	£51,141	£45,753	£56,073	£59,862	£61,814	£52,910
Long-term Liabilities	£0	£50,000	£50,000	£50,000	£50,000	£50,000	£50,000	£50,000	£50,000	£50,000	£50,000	£50,000	£50,000
Total Liabilities	£350	£57,706	£58,234	£80,510	£85,416	£91,541	£107,892	£101,141	£95,753	£106,073	£109,862	£111,814	£102,910
Paid-in Capital	£50,000	£50,000	£50,000	£50,000	£50,000	£50,000	£50,000	£50,000	£50,000	£50,000	£50,000	£50,000	£50,000
Retained Earnings	(£18,350)	(£18,350)	(£18,350)	(£18,350)	(£18,350)	(£18,350)	(£18,350)	(£18,350)	(£18,350)	(£18,350)	(£18,350)	(£18,350)	(£18,350)
Earnings	£0	(£12,328)	(£24,055)	(£28,908)	(£25,885)	(£9,213)	£16,973	£28,158	£30,193	£48,698	£70,540	£95,195	£97,013
Total Capital	£31,650	£19,323	£7,595	£2,743	£5,765	£22,438	£48,623	£59,808	£61,843	£80,348	£102,190	£126,845	£128,663
Total Liabilities and Capital	£32,000	£77,028	£65,829	£83,253	£91,181	£113,979	£156,515	£160,948	£157,596	£186,421	£212,052	£238,659	£231,573
Net Worth	£31,650	£19,323	£7,595	£2,743	£5,765	£22,438	£48,623	£59,808	£61,843	£80,348	£102,190	£126,845	£128,663

AIDA	Acronym for Attention, Interest, Desire, Action.
assets	Items of value belonging to an individual or organization.
balance sheet	A financial snapshot of your business.
break-even point	The point at which revenue equals costs.
capital	The property, equipment and money used for a business.
cash flow statement	A financial statement showing how a business will operate over time.
consultancy	One or more people offering their expertise to others.
co-operative	A group of people operating a business on an equal footing.
copyright	Sole right to reproduce a creative work.
Critical Path Analysis (CPA)	The shortest path through a process ensuring everything gets completed.
depreciation	Decline in value of assets with long-term lives such as plant or machinery.
desk research	Gathering secondary data.
DPA	The Data Protection Act safeguards the right of individuals to have any data recorded about them be accurately recorded and gives them the right to see copies of it. If individuals ask that their names be removed from customer databases, this must be done.
Enterprise Agency	Agencies set up by individual councils to help small businesses.

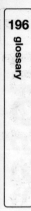

Enterprise Investment Scheme	A tax scheme where investors can invest up to a £150,000 in an unquoted company by buying shares in that company.
factor	Somebody who transacts business on behalf of someone else.
factoring	Buying up trade debts or lending money against security on trade debts.
field research	Gathering original data.
finance house	A company providing loans against security.
franchise	Business offering the right to trade under the parent company name.
KISS	Acronym for 'Keep It Short and Sweet', or 'Keep It Simple, Stupid!'
limited company	A separate legal business entity.
marketing	Assessing customer needs and promoting, distributing and developing the product or service to meet them.
market research	Gathering relevant data by the most appropriate means.
patent	A right of ownership granted to a new invention.
partnership	Ownership where two or more individuals have liability for all the business's debts.
profit and loss forecast	A statement showing whether a business will make a profit or loss over a specific period.
sole trader	An individual who owns and operates a business on his or her own.
SMART	Acronym for Specific, Measurable, Attainable, Relevant, Time-related.
SWOT	An acronym for Strengths, Weaknesses, Opportunities, Threats.
VAT (Value Added Tax)	Indirect tax on products and services.

Chapter 1

1 A document describing your business and suggesting future progress.
2 Short-term to get aid; long-term to plan progress.
3 Three from: financial aid, grant application, show business viability, find strengths and weaknesses, encourage partners, guide employees, help decision-making, guide future action, internal communication, guide development, highlight problems, plan resources, beat competition, make best use of assets, analyse product or service, guide progress, provide overview, concentrate thinking, impress buyers, get regulatory approval.
4 Business description, business type, management, market and marketing, operations, finances, objectives.
5 Make decisions for you, predict the future, improve information.
6 You are the best person to write your own business plan.

Chapter 2

1 Sole trader, partnership, limited company.
2 Consultancy, co-operative, franchise.
3 Companies House.
4 UK Patent Office.
5 70 years from the creator's death.
6 Specific, Measurable, Attainable, Realistic, Timely.
7 Security.

Chapter 3

1 Unique Selling Point.
2 Use a spider diagram.

3   SWOT analysis – Strengths, Weaknesses, Opportunities, Threats.
4   Two from: controlling the whole process, controlling the image, one-to-one relationship with the customer, planning without interference.

Chapter 4

1   Market research involves gathering, analysing, interpreting and presenting data in an organized way.
2   Five from: geography, residence, education, likes and dislikes, disposable income, jobs, family, buying methods, buying habits, buying preferences.
3   Segmentation is choosing a specific group by specific criteria.
4   Four from: interviews, questionnaires, observation, market testing, secondary sources.
5   Customer satisfaction.
6   Benchmarking.
7   Potential customers × (number of product/service per year per customer × price of product service)

Chapter 5

1   Market size, prices, competition, technology.
2   Social, political, economic, government.
3   Product, Price, Promotion, Place.
4   Five from: setting up costs, economies of scale, ongoing costs, making your product different, distribution, legalities, market reactions, brand recognition, location, scarce resources, technology.
5   Field research (original data) and desk research (secondary data).
6   Five: R&D, launch, growth, saturation, death.
7   Attention, Interest, Desire, Action.

Chapter 6

1   Yourself.
2   Operational, technical, financial, marketing, human resources.
3   Sabbaticals, promotion, benefits, holidays, shares, company cars.
4   Franchise.
5   Appraisal and monitoring.

Chapter 7

1   Operations, record-keeping, secretarial, office equipment.

2 Three from: planning consent, listed building consent, building regulations, access, fire safety.
3 Equipment/plant, IT hardware, television and recording equipment, vehicles, furniture, buildings, cleaning machines.
4 Costs, availability, timing, reliability.
5 Critical Path Analysis (CPA).

Chapter 8

1 Cash flow forecast, balance sheet, profit and loss statement.
2 The money generated from selling your product or service.
3 Put a deficit amount in brackets.
4 Double-entry bookkeeping.
5 Assets, liabilities, owners' equity.
6 Unrealistic forecasts, false assumptions.
7 The point where sales income covers the production/buying costs and related operating costs.

Chapter 9

1 Coverage, preparation and implementation.
2 One year.
3 Five years.
4 Break it down into smaller stages.
5 Any legal or regulatory duties.

Chapter 10

1 'Keep it short and simple' (or 'keep it simple, stupid!')
2 Read your work on paper from the bottom of each page to the top.
3 Executive summary.
4 Third person.
5 References.
6 Appendices.

Chapter 11

1 Applying for financial or other aid and running your business.
2 Two from: showing the way forward, monitoring performance, co-coordinating control, communication, empowering staff, generating ideas.
3 Until business circumstances change and you make a new one.
4 You, or you and your business partners.
5 Executive summary.

Useful organizations

British Chambers of Commerce website: www.chamberonline.co.uk

British Franchise Association – Thames View, Newtown Road, Henley-on-Thames, Oxon. RG9 1HG UK; tel: 01491 578050; fax: 01491 573517; e-mail: mailroom@british-franchise.org.uk; Internet: british-franchise.org.uk

British Venture Capital Association – website: www.bvca.co.uk

Business in the Community – 137 Shepherdess Walk, London N1 7RQ; tel: 0870 600 2482; e-mail: information@bitc.org.uk; website: www.bitc.org.uk

Business Link (England) – tel: 0845-600 9606; website: www.businesslink.org

Business Eye (Wales) – tel: 0845-796 9798; website: www.businesseye.org.uk; e-mail: assistance@businesseye.org.uk

Business Gateway (Scotland) – tel: 0845-609 6611; website: www.bgateway.com

Chartered Institute of Marketing – Moor Hall, Cookham, Maidenhead, Berkshire SL6 9QH; tel: 01628 427500; fax : 01628 427499; e-mail: info@cim.co.uk; website: www.cim.co.uk

Companies House – Main Office, Crown Way, Maindy, Cardiff CF14 3UZ; tel: 0870 33 33 636, e-mail: enquiries@companies-house.gov.uk; website: www.companieshouse.gov.uk

Department for Work and Pensions – Correspondence Unit, Room 540, The Adelphi, 1–11 John Adam Street, London WC2N 6HT; tel: 020 7712 2171 (9.00 am–5.00 pm Monday–Friday); fax: 020 7712 2386; website: www.dwp.gov.uk

Enterprise Investment Scheme – website: www.inlandrevenue.gov.uk/pdfs/ir137.htm

Federation of Small Businesses – website: www.fsb.org.uk

Health and Safety Executive – website: www.hse.gov.uk

Information Commissioner's Office – Wycliffe House, Water Lane, Wilmslow, Cheshire SK9 5AF; fax: 01625 524 510; Data Protection Help Line (first time of contact) tel: 01625 545 745; e-mail: mail@ico.gsi.gov.uk; general tel: 01625 545 700; e-mail: mail@ico.gsi.gov.uk; website: www.informationcommissioner.gov.uk

Inland Revenue – website: www.inlandrevenue.gov.uk

The Institute of Direct Marketing – 1 Park Road, Teddington, Middlesex TW11 0AR; tel: 020 8977 5705; fax: 020 8943 2535; e-mail: enquiries@theidm.com; website: www.theidm.co.uk

Institute of Insurance Brokers – Higham Business Centre, Midland Road, Higham Ferrers, Northamptonshire NN10 8DW; tel: 01933 410 003; e-mail: inst.ins.brokers@iib-uk.com; website: www.iib-uk.com

Invest Northern Ireland – 44–58 May Street, Belfast BT1 4NN; tel: 028 9023 9090; fax: 028 9049 0490; e-mail: info@investni.com; website: www.investni.com

The Market Research Society – 15 Northburgh Street, London EC1V 0JR; tel: 020 7490 4911; fax: 020 7490 0608; e-mail: info@mrs.org.uk; website: www.mrs.org.uk

Office of Fair Trading – Fleetbank House, 2–6 Salisbury Square, London EC4Y 8JX; tel: 08457 22 44 99; e-mail: enquiries@oft.gsi.gov.uk; website: www.oft.gov.uk

Prince's Youth Trust – Head Office, 18 Park Square East, London NW1 4LH; tel: 020 7543 1234; fax: 020 7543 1200; minicom

0207 543 1374; e-mail webinfops@princes-trust.org.uk; website: www.princes-trust.org.uk

Small Firms Loan Guarantee Scheme – tel: 0845 001 0032/33

Trading Standards Office – www.tradingstandards.gov.uk

UK Patent Office – Main Office, Concept House, Cardiff Road, Newport, South Wales NP10 8QQ; tel: 08459 500 505 (charged at local rate); e-mail: enquiries@patent.gov.uk; website: www.patent.gov.uk/

Useful websites

Some of these sites provide free business plan templates, sample business plans or advice on writing plans. Non-UK versions can easily be adapted to UK standards.
www.acoa.ca/e/business/business_plan/index.shtml – business plan outline
www.bcentral.co.uk/issues/startingup/default.mspx – advice for start-up businesses
www.bplans.com/sp/businessplans.cfm – free sample business plans
www.clearlybusiness.com – Barclays Bank business information
www.business-plan-help.com/writing-a-business-plan-examples.html – example of how to write a business plan
www.entrepreneur.com/graphics/sampleplan.pdf – example business plan
www.innovation-dynamics.co.uk/innovateur.co.uk_plans.html – business plan advice and business plan templates
www.mindtools.com/critpath.html – how to do a Critical Path Analysis
http://www.planware.org/busplan.htm – free business plan template
www.rbs.co.uk/Small_Business/Starting_Your_Business/default.htm – Royal Bank of Scotland advice on starting a business
http://www.startinbusiness.co.uk/flowchart/4flowchart_businessplans.htm – how to write a business plan
www.teneric.co.uk/business-plan-outline.html – business plan advcie and outline

Business plan software

BizHelp24 – www.bizhelp24.com/services/software_books/business_software.shtml
BPlans – www.bplans.com
Exl-Plan – www.planware.org/exlplan.htm
Palo Alto, Business Plan Pro 2004 – http://paloalto.co.uk
Plan IT Business Plan 3, Life Software – www.lifesoftware.com
Teneric, Business Plan Express – www.teneric.co.uk/business-plan.html
WinForecast Professional Editions – www.winforecast.com.au

Further reading

Colin Barrow, Paul Barrow and Robert Brown, *The Business Plan Workbook* (Kogan Page, 2001)

Sally Bingwood and Melissa Spore, *Presenting Numbers, Tables, and Charts* (OUP, 2003)

Polly Bird, *Market Research in a Week* (Hodder & Stoughton, 2003)

Polly Bird, *Teach Yourself Time Management* (Hodder & Stoughton, 2002)

Edward Blackwell, *How to Prepare a Business Plan* (Kogan Page, 2004)

Brian Finch, *How to Write a Business Plan* (Kogan Page, 2001)

Alexander Hiam, *Marketing for Dummies* (HIAM, 2004)

Ron Johnson, *The 24 Hour Business Plan* (Random House, ebooks, 2002)

Ian Maitland, *Successful Business Plans in a Week* (Hodder & Stoughton, 1998)

Richard Milton, *Do Your Own PR* (Pocket Essentials, 2003)

Linda Pinson, *Anatomy of a Business Plan* (USA, Dearborn Trade Publishing, 2004)

Matthew Record, *Preparing a Winning Business Plan* (How to Books, 2003)

Jonathan Reuvid, Roderick Millar, *Start Up and Run Your Own Business* (Kogan Page, 2004)

Hal Schaeffer, *Essentials of Cash Flow* (John Wiley & Sons, 2002)

Richard Stutely, *The Definitive Business Plan* (Prentice Hall, 2001)

Declan Treacy, Polly Bird, *Successful Time Management in a Week* (Hodder & Stoughton, 2003)

Alan West, *A Business Plan* (Prentice Hall, 1998)

John Whitely, *Going for Self-Employment: How to Set up and Run Your own Business* (How To Books, 2003)

| teach yourself | **setting up a small business** |
| | vera hughes & david weller |

- Are you setting up a small business?
- Do you need help to define your product or service?
- Are you looking for guidance in marketing and finance?

Setting Up a Small Business helps you with all the everyday aspects of running a small business and gives detailed guidance on specialized areas such as legal requirements, opening a retail or office-based business, staff selection and marketing.

Vera Hughes and **David Weller** started their own business in 1980, having been involved in the retail industry for many years. They have written a number of books on retailing.

teach yourself	**marketing** j. jonathan gabay

- Do you want to understand the principles of marketing?
- Do you need to promote your business, product or organization more effectively?
- Are you looking for more creative marketing ideas?

Marketing concentrates on the engine which drives successful marketing – imagination. Revealing many profitable tips and secrets to help you target, brand and sell your enterprise whilst generating provocative publicity, this book will keep you three steps ahead of the competition.

J. Jonathan Gabay is an award-winning copywriter, course director at the Chartered Institute of Marketing, the world's biggest marketing training organization, and director of a creative marketing consultancy firm.

teach yourself

finance for non-financial managers
phiłip ramsden

- Do you need to understand your company's financial reports?
- Do you want to know what financial accounts really mean?
- Do you need to understand accounting jargon?

Finance for Non-Financial Managers strips away the mystery from finance and accountancy and allows you to ask pertinent questions and understand the answers. With detailed explanations and practical examples, the world of finance is mapped out steadily and clearly.

Philip Ramsden SA, MDA, MA, FCMM has worked in accounting and systems development in various sections of business, from the dairy industry to metals recycling.